A Note From Denise Renner

The Word of God is so powerful in our lives. It is essential that every person spend time with God and study His Word in order to stay spiritually strong in these last days.

This study guide corresponds to my *TIME With Denise Renner* TV program by the same title that can be viewed at **deniserenner.org**. My desire is that through these lessons, you find the encouragement and freedom in Christ that you need. I believe the Holy Spirit is going to speak to you through the words you read in this study tool and that as you begin to use it, you will be *propelled* into the abundant life God has planned for you. I encourage you to make the effort to receive all He has for you and all He wants to do in you — it will definitely be worth it!

Whether you have walked with the Lord a long time or have just begun to follow Him, there is so much He wants to give you from His Word. He sees where you are, and He wants to meet you there.

> **Therefore do not worry about tomorrow, for tomorrow will worry about its own things. Sufficient for the day is its own trouble.**
> **— Matthew 6:34**

Your sister and friend in Jesus Christ,

Denise Renner

Maintaining Peace in Difficult Times

TOPIC

Maintaining Peace by the Power of Forgiveness

SCRIPTURES

1. **John 10:10** — The thief does not come except to steal, and to kill, and to destroy. I have come that they may have life, and that they may have *it* more abundantly.

2. **Mark 11:25** — And whenever you stand praying, if you have anything against anyone, forgive him, that your Father in heaven may also forgive you your trespasses.

3. **Acts 7:55-60** — But he, being full of the Holy Spirit, gazed into heaven and saw the glory of God, and Jesus standing at the right hand of God, and said, "Look! I see the heavens opened and the Son of Man standing at the right hand of God!" Then they cried out with a loud voice, stopped their ears, and ran at him with one accord; and they cast *him* out of the city and stoned *him*. And the witnesses laid down their clothes at the feet of a young man named Saul. And they stoned Stephen as he was calling on *God* and saying, "Lord Jesus, receive my spirit." Then he knelt down and cried out with a loud voice, "Lord, do not charge them with this sin." And when he had said this, he fell asleep.

4. **Luke 23:34** — Then Jesus said, "Father, forgive them, for they do not know what they do." And they divided His garments and cast lots.

5. **Luke 23:46** — And when Jesus had cried out with a loud voice, He said, "Father, 'into Your hands I commit My spirit.'" Having said this, He breathed His last.

6. **Romans 5:5** — Now hope does not disappoint, because the love of God has been poured out in our hearts by the Holy Spirit who was given to us.

7. **Matthew 18:21,22** — Then Peter came to Him and said, "Lord, how often shall my brother sin against me, and I forgive him? Up to seven times?" Jesus said to him, "I do not say to you, up to seven times, but up to seventy times seven."

SYNOPSIS

The 15 lessons in this study on *Maintaining Peace in Difficult Times* will focus on the following topics:

- Maintaining Peace by the Power of Forgiveness
- Maintaining Peace by Controlling Your Emotions
- Maintaining Peace by Choosing To Be Thankful
- Maintaining Peace by Seeing Your Problem as Smaller Than God!
- Maintaining Peace by Knowing the Lover on the Inside
- Maintaining Peace by Knowing the Comforter
- Maintaining Peace by Refusing the Trap of Isolation
- Maintaining Peace by Making a Habit of Rejoicing
- Maintaining Peace by Giving Your Worries to God
- Maintaining Peace by Recognizing the Real Enemy
- Maintaining Peace by Living One Day at a Time
- Maintaining Peace by Guarding Your Thoughts
- Maintaining Peace by Controlling Your Mouth
- Maintaining Peace by Controlling Your Mouth AGAIN
- Maintaining Peace by Remembering What God Has Already Done for You

Nothing steals our peace faster than a bitter grudge over a past hurt. That's why it's so important that we make the conscious, purposeful choice to forgive — when we don't, unforgiveness will rob us of our peace. But when we choose to go to God with our hurts, receive His healing and the grace to forgive, and release the people who hurt us, we can maintain our peace in the middle of challenges and wield our peace as a weapon against the enemy.

The emphasis of this lesson:

One of the main ways Satan tries to steal our peace is through the trap of offense and unforgiveness. But with God's help, we can forgive quickly, avoid the enemy's traps, and maintain our peace in difficult times.

To Maintain Peace, We Need To Forgive

In the day and culture that we're living in right now, one of the most crucial skills we need to develop is *how to maintain our peace in difficult times.*

The Bible says that as we get closer to Jesus' coming, it's not going to get any easier, which means we have to be well-equipped in maintaining our peace. It is *so* important to be prepared to stay in peace in troubled times. And in order for us to maintain our peace, we need desperately to remember the power of God's presence on the inside of us and to keep an attitude of forgiveness towards others, even in the most difficult circumstance.

Why do you think that this is such a powerful key to hold on to? When you're holding on to an attitude of offense, unforgiveness, or bitterness, it has a way of stealing your peace. But when you give the gift of forgiveness, it opens the door for you to experience the unshakeable peace of God that Jesus died to give you.

On the program, Denise shared several testimonies of people who have told her, "I didn't think I could forgive. What had happened to me was so terrible...but when I did forgive, it was like a huge weight came off my shoulders and off my heart, and I was able to move forward." Some of them even restored the relationship that had been broken for so many years.

The Enemy Uses Unforgiveness To Steal, Kill, and Destroy

The last thing the enemy wants is for you to experience God's peace. In fact, he wants to do anything he can to disrupt or steal it from you. John 10:10 (*KJV*) says:

> **The thief cometh not, but for to steal, and to kill, and to destroy: I [Jesus] am come that they might have life, and that they might have it more abundantly.**

Satan wants to steal, kill, and destroy your ability to experience the great peace that's inside you by the Holy Spirit, but you don't have to yield to his destructive ways.

Denise knows what it feels like to overcome bitterness and unforgiveness. For two whole years many years ago, horrible emotions brought deep fear to her mind and soul and even created problems in her body. Her hands, her feet, and even her face became painfully cold all the time. She had so much fear and she was so desperate for peace that she began to seek God with all of her heart.

Maybe you're reading this right now and you're thinking to yourself, *I so much want to be calm and at peace.* Well, friend, the first step toward the peace you crave is letting go of any unforgiveness and bitterness that's been hiding in your heart.

You might think, *I have a right to these emotions!* But as long as you hold on to that mindset, those emotions will stay with you; only they won't stay just as they are right now. Over time, they'll become more deeply ingrained in your soul and personality, giving the enemy opportunity to do what he wants to do: "steal, kill, and destroy" you from the inside out.

As Denise was stuck in this mindset herself, reading the Word, seeking the Lord, and wanting peace, she eventually realized that her problem was *not* the person she was angry with. She shared the following:

> I came to understand it wasn't about the other person. It was about *me*, and it was about my relationship with God. God wanted to teach me that I could be free and that I could set others free from the prison of unforgiveness I had held them in by forgiving them. And I'm telling you right now, if we want to maintain peace in these difficult times, one of the things we're all going to have to have is the knowledge and the conviction to forgive.

Peace Is a Powerful Weapon

The Word of God is so powerful, and peace is powerful. Some people look at peace like it's just a passive thing, but peace is anything but passive. Peace is actually active and assertive, and it's a major part of our spiritual protection.

In fact, when the apostle Paul describes our spiritual armor and weapons through the analogy of the Roman soldier in Ephesians 6, he includes peace in that list. And he describes it as our foundation, as our *shoes* of peace. Why do you think they were called shoes of peace? Because on the bottom of those shoes were spikes. If an army of Roman soldiers marched down the street, anyone who stood in their way would be run over with those spikes. Those are the spiritual shoes that you have on your feet to give you a solid foundation as you fight Satan's attacks.

Do you see what a great weapon your peace is? When anxiety is plaguing your mind, peace comes and takes authority and says through you, "Worry, be quiet! Fear, you're not touching me now! I'm going to enjoy my day. I'm going to enjoy my family. I am taking hold of the peace of God that's on the inside of me. I am recognizing these shoes of peace on my feet."

When we received Jesus into our heart as Lord and Savior, He outfitted us with this mighty piece of stabilizing armor against the enemy. And in order to use that armor and hold on to our peace, we have to learn how to forgive and release others.

As Denise stated on the program, as long as she remained in a place of bitterness and unforgiveness, she had no peace. But when she learned that she needed to forgive and made the choice to do so, she had a miracle in her life. The next day her hands were normal, her feet were normal, and most of all, her mind was normal again!

What happened? That powerful step of forgiveness opened the door so she could once again experience — not just read about — the peace that passes all understanding (*see* Philippians 4:6). When we give the gift of forgiveness to others, by freeing them in our own hearts, we can experience that peace for ourselves.

One of the most impactful examples of this truth is the story of Stephen in Acts 7. He was the first martyr of the Church. He had been preaching, which enraged a huge crowd of Jews to the point that they decided they wanted to stone him.

The Bible says that in that crowd was a young man named Saul. When we continue to read the book of Acts, we learn that this young man Saul, who was involved in the stoning of Stephen was the future apostle Paul. And as Stephen was dying without cause at the hands of people who were falsely accusing him, brutally killing him, he said, "Lord Jesus, receive my spirit" (v. 59). Then he got down on his knees and cried out, "Father, do not hold this charge against them" (v. 60).

WOW. Stephen was berated, ridiculed, and hated, and now he was being murdered. And in that last moment, with those last breaths that he had in his lungs, he was *forgiving* every person that was guilty of taking part in his murder, including the man who would become the apostle Paul. And Stephen chose to free them from any unforgiveness he could have held on to. Does this remind you of someone else?

Think of Jesus on the Cross, bleeding from every place on His body. Picture His arms stretched out with nails in His hands, His joints strained as He fought to take even small breaths. For Him to breathe, He had to push up on the nails that were in His feet.

As the crowd is blaspheming Him, He's suffering. He's carrying all the weight, all the sin of mankind — past, present, and future. He's carrying hate, murder, and every disease known to man. He's carrying anything that would come against you to steal your peace. It's all happening in that moment on the Cross. And in that moment as He's dying and fighting every spiritual battle on our behalf, He cries out to the Father in Luke 23:34 (*NIV*) and says:

> ... **"Father, forgive them, for they do not know what they are doing."** ...

Then verse 46 says:

> ... **"Father, into your hands I commit my spirit." When he had said this, he breathed his last.**

If we could go back in time and stand in that crowd, we might have said, "Of course they know what they're doing!" But in the heart and mind of Jesus on that Cross — He's the one experiencing our pain and sin as He hears their blasphemous words — they were completely ignorant of their wrong actions.

If Jesus — the only perfect One to ever exist — extended forgiveness as He was being brutally and unfairly murdered, don't we have every responsibility to pass on that forgiveness to the people who hurt us?

There are two other vitally important reasons to forgive. The first is, if we want to experience peace in our own heart, we have to come to the place where we say, "I can't have this anymore. I cannot bear the turmoil of having these negative thoughts and attitudes. I can no longer stand to ignore that person and act like he or she is not alive. I refuse to continue this pattern. I know I need to forgive."

Jesus shares the second reason with us in Mark 11:25 and 26:

And whenever you stand praying, if you have anything against anyone, forgive him, that your Father in heaven may also forgive you your trespasses. But if you do not forgive, neither will your Father in heaven forgive your trespasses.

Denise understood that she needed God's forgiveness, so she needed to forgive. You might be reading this lesson and thinking, *I understand what you're saying, but you don't know what those people did to me. I've carried this hurt for so long, and I haven't spoken to them for years. I don't want them in my life. I don't even want to say their name or remember the relationship we used to have. How can I do this?*

God Has Equipped You To Forgive

If these thoughts are plaguing you, we have good news for you: If you are a believer in Jesus Christ, when you were born again, something amazing happened on the inside of you. Romans 5:5 (*KJV*) explains it this way:

…The love of God is shed abroad in our hearts by the Holy Ghost which is given unto us.

When the Holy Spirit came to live in your heart, He brought the resurrection power of Jesus. He brought His very self and the perfect love of God into your soul. He placed there the exact love that He loves you with today and that He's going to love you with in eternity. This is the love that God the Father loved Jesus with — *that same exact love* is inside your heart.

This means we have the same exact equipment inside us that we need to forgive anyone for whatever he or she did to hurt us. You might ask, "How many times do I have to forgive?" Peter asked that same question in Matthew 18:21 (*NIV*), "… 'Lord, how many times shall I forgive my brother or sister who sins against me? Up to seven times?'"

Jesus answered with an astonishing command, "I do not say to you, up to seven times, but up to seventy times seven" (*see* Matthew 18:22). This amounts to 490 times! Jesus was saying, "You forgive until I come back. You forgive until you go to the grave."

If we want to maintain peace in these difficult times, we're going to have to have a conviction and an understanding, a pattern we continually repeat in our heart:

- *I'm going to forgive.*
- *I'm going to become an intentional forgiver.*
- *I refuse to carry bitterness and unforgiveness in my soul.*
- *I'm going to recognize the love of God on the inside of me.*
- *I'm going to give the same forgiveness and love to others that God gave me through His Son, Jesus.*

Think of how much peace and power that will bring to your life and relationships! While bitterness and unforgiveness opens the door for the enemy to come into your life to steal, kill and destroy, forgiveness opens the door to Heaven's best in your life. It opens the door for you to experience the peace and power of the love of God that's inside you. To give the same mercy to someone else that's been given to us is one of the most beautiful ways to reflect the love of Christ.

We need to know how to maintain our peace through forgiveness, not only for our own heart, but also for the people around us. There are so many people walking around on this planet in torment and turmoil on the inside because they've been wounded; they don't know what to do with their wounds and they don't know how to forgive. They might be people at the grocery store or in your workplace. They might be your relatives. Whoever they are, they might be so worried about relationships that are falling apart or what they're currently experiencing in life. We're all plagued by stress in some form, but when we can maintain the peace of God on the inside of us in the midst of that stress, it can truly transform relationships. Showing others the love and mercy of God may be just what they need at that moment.

Denise's prayer for you:

Father, right now I pray with my friends. I know that they can see that person in their mind's eye — they can hear the name of the person that they need to forgive. And, Father, right now, by our own will, we agree with the power of the Holy Spirit and Your love on the inside of us, and we let that person go. We forgive that individual and choose to be like Jesus and say, "Father, forgive them — they didn't know what they were doing. Thank You for forgiving me for holding on to any bitterness or unforgiveness that I've had in my heart. I thank You for the power of Your forgiveness that's inside me and for the peace that I will get to experience as a result of forgiveness. I pray this in Jesus' name, amen."

STUDY QUESTIONS

**Be diligent to present yourself approved to God, a worker
who does not need to be ashamed, rightly dividing the word of truth.**
— 2 Timothy 2:15

1. On the program, Denise shared the power of her choice to forgive. When she forgave, her life went from torment to peace, even in the midst of difficulties. What parable did Jesus tell that illustrates the connection between forgiveness and peace (*see* Matthew 18:21-35)?

2. How do you think Stephen, like Jesus, could forgive his murderers AS they were murdering him? Take a look at First John 5:19, Matthew 10:5-8, and Hebrews 12:2 for the answer.

3. What kind of forgiveness has God the Father shown to us? (*Hint*: Read Luke 15:11-32 for a stunning picture of the way He has forgiven you personally.)

PRACTICAL APPLICATION

**But be doers of the word,
and not hearers only, deceiving yourselves.**
— James 1:22

1. Do you find yourself constantly frustrated or dealing with negative mental, emotional, or even physical symptoms…for seemingly no reason? If so, do you think it could be stemming from an undealt-with grudge? If so, ask God to show you who you need to forgive and how you can begin to release them, pray for them, and move forward.

2. Have you ever had a friend who was poisoned by bitterness? How did that person's decision to choose bitterness instead of forgiveness affect his or her relationships with others? What are some ways that choosing forgiveness would impact that person differently?

3. Take another look at Romans 5:5. What do you think it means to have the love of God in your heart? What would that look like? List some practical ways you can display God's love toward those around you.

TOPIC

Maintaining Peace by Controlling Your Emotions

SCRIPTURES

1. **1 Corinthians 10:13** — No temptation has overtaken you except such as is common to man; but God is faithful, who will not allow you to be tempted beyond what you are able, but with the temptation will also make the way of escape, that you may be able to bear it.

2. **Hebrews 4:15,16** — For we do not have a High Priest who cannot sympathize with our weaknesses, but was in all points tempted as we are, yet without sin. Let us therefore come boldly to the throne of grace, that we may obtain mercy and find grace to help in time of need.

3. **Matthew 6:26** — Look at the birds of the air, for they neither sow nor reap nor gather into barns; yet your heavenly Father feeds them. Are you not of more value than they?

4. **Luke 12:24** — Consider the ravens, for they neither sow nor reap, which have neither storehouse nor barn; and God feeds them. Of how much more value are you than the birds?

5. **1 Peter 5:7** (*AMPC*) — Casting the whole of your care [all your anxieties, all your worries, all your concerns, once and for all] on Him, for He cares for you affectionately and cares about you watchfully.

6. **Philippians 4:5** — Let your gentleness be known to all men. The Lord is at hand.

7. **Hebrews 12:2** (*AMPC*) — Looking away [from all that will distract] to Jesus, Who is the Leader and the Source of our faith [giving the first incentive for our belief] and is also its Finisher [bringing it to maturity and perfection]. He, for the joy [of obtaining the prize] that was set before Him, endured the cross, despising and ignoring the shame, and is now seated at the right hand of the throne of God.

8. **Proverbs 16:32** — He who is slow to anger is better than the mighty, and he who rules his spirit than he who takes a city.

SYNOPSIS

One of the most important lessons for every believer to learn is the habit of keeping our emotions in check. When we let emotions control our lives, they will keep us tossing to and fro on the waves of the situations we find ourselves in. However, when we choose to lead our lives with the wisdom of God's Word instead, we can truly have peace and make progress, even when we're dealing with difficult moments and difficult people.

The emphasis of this lesson:

Emotions make great messengers, but terrible leaders. When we take the initiative to lead our feelings instead of letting them drive our decisions, we can maintain our peace on an everyday basis, even in the face of hard situations.

To Maintain Peace, We Need To Keep Our Emotions in Check

When we choose to maintain our peace in difficult times, we are able to be a huge strength and help to the people around us. They will notice something different about us when they're depressed, afraid, or anxious but they see us remain steady and peaceful. We can be a truly powerful example of hope, and the Lord has called us to that kind of life. He wants us to know and understand, experience and hold on to the amazing fruit of peace that He's placed in us, even in the midst of troubling circumstances.

Denise shared on the program about a lady in her meeting who had a vision of a tornado, and how she was in the eye of the tornado — in the very center — and there was absolute peace. Even with many of the crazy situations going on around us, current events on the news, relational problems, physical problems, financial problems…They are like the winds of a tornado swirling around us, but in the middle — right in the middle — there's great peace.

Like an anchor, the Holy Spirit on the inside of you can give you that kind of unshakeable peace to keep you stable through life's challenges. In those difficult times — and the Bible says they may get worse — it's critically important that we know even more *how to maintain our peace.*

One verse points out some very good news for us to know. The Bible says when we see difficult things happening, "… Look up and lift up your heads, because your redemption draws near" (*see* Luke 21:28.) If we start seeing many of these things such as earthquakes, wars, famines, hatred, rebellious children, and relationship problems, we can know Jesus is coming back very soon (*see* Matthew 24).

As we are talking about maintaining our peace in difficult times, one step that we can take towards peace is by controlling our emotions instead of letting them control us. It's such a powerful position to be in charge of our emotions. Sometimes it is very challenging, but the power of God through the fruit of self-control on the inside of you is greater than the storm that's working around you, so know that you can manage them well.

You Are Not Alone in This Struggle

God created us with emotions that reflect a part of who He is. Emotions serve a purpose in our lives, but they can affect us in negative ways if not handled properly. All of us are tempted to let our feelings take the lead in our lives on occasion. Often the devil will say something to us like, "This is the worst. Nobody else understands what you're going through. You can't make it through this." When he tries to bring you down with thoughts like these, remember First Corinthians 10:13:

> **No temptation has overtaken you except such as is common to man; but God is faithful, who will not allow you to be tempted beyond what you are able, but with the temptation will also make the way of escape, that you may be able to bear it.**

This verse says that every temptation that tries to overtake us is commonly experienced by all believers; the same temptation that comes to you also comes to others, and vice versa. We all have temptations come to us as a result of negative thoughts because of what somebody said or didn't say, or what somebody did or didn't do.

The temptation to harbor anger, frustration, jealousy, and even envy, come to all of us in some way at some time, but the good news is that we don't have to yield to those things.

Hebrews 4:15 and 16 says that Jesus was tempted in all ways as we are, so He understands and can identify with our temptation, yet He didn't sin. So being tempted in and of itself is never sin, but giving a place to that temptation is. Thankfully, Jesus gives us the power to overcome it (*see* 1 Corinthians 10:13), even when our emotions threaten to steal our peace and push us into a wrong decision.

When we spend enough time with the Holy Spirit, who is the representation of Jesus on the earth, we begin to act the way He does. Peace, or tranquility, is one of His emotions. He is never anxious, worried, or fearful, so we don't have to be either.

Denise mentioned that sometimes she is tempted to worry about things, which definitely robs her of peace. The Holy Spirit said to her, "Denise, stop worrying about this." When she thought about Him and how He is inside her, she realized He was not having a nervous breakdown because of what was happening. He was actually very, very calm, and because of that, she could also be calm.

That's the power of the peace of God on the inside of *you*. When you're in that place, you can hold on to the peace He's given you and learn to manage your emotions instead of letting them have control over you.

Look at the Birds

Jesus said in Matthew 6:26 and in Luke 12:24 to look at the birds. When you look further into the Greek of that phrase, it means to *consider, think about, or examine*. Why should we examine the birds? Because they don't fret or worry about anything — not even food — yet our Heavenly Father feeds them.

Have you ever seen birds sitting on a telephone wire, or perched in a tree, having a nervous breakdown, worried sick about where their next worm will come from? No, of course not. Why? Because the same God who spoke the stars into existence and rained down manna for the Israelites in the desert takes care of every sparrow.

After Jesus told us to look at the birds, He asked, "Are you not of more value than they?" (*see* Matthew 6:26). In case you are wondering, YES, you are. Your Heavenly Father adores you and wants to take care of your needs (*see* Philippians 4:19; 2 Corinthians 9:8).

As God is instructing us in His Word, there's an example even in the birds for us to follow. Many people may not care much about birds, but there's One that does and that is our Heavenly Father. And He says to YOU, His child:

If I care about and feed those birds, you can be sure I will care for you, son.

You can be sure I will provide for you, daughter.

The Bible promises we can cast all of our cares — every single worry and concern we have — upon the Lord, because He cares for us. First Peter 5:7 (*AMPC*) says:

> **Casting the whole of your care [all your anxieties, all your worries, all your concerns, once and for all] on Him, for He cares for you affectionately and cares about you watchfully.**

He cares about every single detail that's going on in your life, and as you recognize His care, it will help you have peace in the midst of difficult moments. When you are tempted to worry, it will help you slow down and say, "No, I'm not going to get upset about this. No, anger, you will not drive me to lash out. No, worry, I will not yield to you because I'm maintaining my peace."

You Can Have Peace in the Middle of Hard Times

When the apostle Paul was writing the book of Philippians, he was in a terrible place, in a nasty prison. At this point, he could have had all kinds of negative emotions swirling around inside him, but instead he had peace, and he was rejoicing. In Philippians 4:5, Paul advised us:

> **Let your gentleness** [moderation] **be known to all men.** [For] **The Lord is at hand.**

Because the Lord is at hand — *He is coming* — this verse tells us that we need to control, manage or rein in our emotions. When Denise read that verse, she visualized sideview mirrors on a car tucking in, so they wouldn't hit the walls when the car is driven into a tight space. This is important so the mirrors can't damage anything outside the car, and what is outside the car can't damage those mirrors.

In the same way, we need to speak to our hearts, to take control of our emotions, to rein or pull them in when we encounter tight situations so that we can pass through them peacefully. Some of the things we can say to calm ourselves are:

- "Worry, be quiet."
- "*NO*, fear. I'm saying 'no' to you disrupting my day."

- "God has not given me a spirit of fear, but of *power* and *love* and a *sound mind*" (*see* 2 Timothy 1:7).
- "I will not worry about tomorrow, because Jesus promised He would take care of me" (*see* Matthew 6:34).

You see, friend, you have the power to take control of your emotions by the Holy Spirit, because He lives on the inside of you, and one of His fruits is self-control (*see* Galatians 5:22,23). When you recognize the power of His presence in you, you'll be able to remain in peace in these difficult times. Hebrews 12:2 (*AMPC*) also reminds us:

> **Looking away [from all that will distract] to Jesus, Who is the Leader and the Source of our faith [giving the first incentive for our belief] and is also its Finisher [bringing it to maturity and perfection]. He, for the joy [of obtaining the prize] that was set before Him, endured the cross, despising and ignoring the shame, and is now seated at the right hand of the throne of God.**

The beginning of this verse talks about where the writer of Hebrews' eyes were, and where our eyes need to be. Jesus was looking forward to the joy of being with you, and Scripture says we need to keep our eyes on Him. We can choose to acknowledge our emotions, but also choose to look and keep our focus on Jesus. Even when we don't know what's going on or what we're supposed to do, we know for sure we can look to Jesus. And when we look to Jesus, the rest of our challenges seem much less intimidating.

Oh, To Be Slow to Anger!

One of the most amazing verses in Scripture is Proverbs 16:32, and it gives us insight into what God says about someone who controls their emotions:

> **He who is slow to anger is better than the mighty, and he who rules** [controls] **his spirit than he who takes a city.**

God says that the one who is slow to anger is better than the mighty. We might have high opinions of people the world considers "mighty," but God says it's more valuable to have self-control than an abundance of money, or a lot of power and influence. When we control our emotions and rein in our anger by the power of the Holy Spirit that's on the inside of us, we can maintain our peace in difficult times.

This verse goes on to make an even stronger statement, that he who rules his spirit is stronger than he who takes a city. Wow!

We look at generals, admirals, great men and women in history and our current day who have authority, sharp military strategy, brilliance of power, influence, or great courage, and we say, "Oh, they're due our honor because they're so powerful." It's not wrong to show honor where honor is due. But in God's eyes, if you control your emotions, you are *more* powerful than a general who won a battle and took a city. This shows us it's not only possible, but highly beneficial for us to learn to rule our spirit.

While that verse was written in the Old Testament, in the New Testament, by the power of the Holy Spirit, we have the fruit of self-control in us. When we say, *"Lord, I don't know how to do this but I'm submitting to You,"* He gives us the grace to act like He does and helps us rein in our emotions like those car mirrors. This is how we can protect ourselves and others while we maintain our peace in difficult times.

This principle is so important in our lives and we must share it with our loved ones. When we submit ourselves to the Holy Spirit, we don't have to lose our minds to runaway emotions — we can have peace and come at every situation from a place of power instead of anxiety. Through the mighty Holy Spirit, we have power that's even greater than the one who can take a city. His presence on the inside of you is like a great general with a great army coming against the forces that are trying to stop you. But you can be unstoppable because the greater One is in you (*see* 1 John 4:4)!

This is why God is calling us to maintain our peace by the power of the Holy Spirit on behalf of ourselves and others.

Denise's prayer for you:

> Father, I thank you for the mighty power of the Holy Spirit on the inside of my friend reading this, and that no matter what we're going through, we have the power You've given us through Your Spirit to take a hold of and maintain our peace in difficult times. Thank You for Your power and promise to never leave us nor forsake us. Thank You that You are not only with us, but You are in us, facing everything we are going through and helping us to keep our peace in difficult times. Thank You, Father, in the precious name of Jesus. Amen.

STUDY QUESTIONS

**Be diligent to present yourself approved to God, a worker
who does not need to be ashamed, rightly dividing the word of truth.
— 2 Timothy 2:15**

1. Reining in our feelings is very important to maintaining peace and operating in wisdom. What are some unwise decisions King Saul made because he couldn't control his emotions (*see* 1 Samuel 13:7-14, 18:7-11, 19:10-12)?

2. Which disciple let his feelings steer him towards attempting murder (*see* John 18:10)? How did Jesus respond (*see* Luke 22:51)?

3. What did Jesus pray when He was overwhelmed with anxiety about facing the Cross (*see* Luke 22:41-44)? What happened as a result?

PRACTICAL APPLICATION

**But be doers of the word,
and not hearers only, deceiving yourselves.
— James 1:22**

1. Which feelings tend to derail you the most? Is it bitterness left over from a past hurt? Frustration from the way your spouse or a co-worker treats you? Anxiety that you won't have what you need? Envy over someone else's success? Ask God to show you which feeling(s) you need to address, and write out what He shows you.

2. What have those feelings driven you to say or do that you wouldn't have if you had managed your emotions? How do you want to do things differently moving forward? Invite the Holy Spirit to begin to empower you to make decisions based on peace instead of emotions, and He will help you to do just that.

TOPIC

Maintaining Peace by Choosing To Be Thankful

SCRIPTURES

1. **1 Thessalonians 5:18** — … In everything give thanks; for this is the will of God in Christ Jesus for you.

2. **Philippians 4:6** — Be anxious for nothing, but in everything by prayer and supplication, with thanksgiving, let your requests be made known to God.

3. **Philippians 2:14,15** — Do all things without complaining and disputing, that you may become blameless and harmless, children of God without fault in the midst of a crooked and perverse generation, among whom you shine as lights in the world.

SYNOPSIS

Did you know that thanking God is one of the fastest ways to calm your heart? When our minds are focused on what we don't have, what we wish we had, or the parts of life that are hard, we're priming our souls to stay in an anxious, doubtful state. That's why it is so important to renew our mind with God's Word, to stay grateful even in difficult circumstances, and to be focused on good things and the blessings He's given us.

The emphasis of this lesson:

Keeping a thankful attitude is one of the best ways to hold on to your peace. Instead of dwelling on the frustrating parts of life, choose to thank God for the ways He has provided for you, times He has protected you, things He has taught you, and people He has placed in your life.

Stay Thankful in Challenging Situations

In the first two lessons, we talked about maintaining our peace in the middle of difficult times, and as we get closer to Jesus coming again, it is even more important because He said there will be greater challenges ahead.

So, how do we do that? How do we hold on to our peace even when people hurt us? Even when things don't go our way? Even when we feel depressed or angry?

We can't just stop going to church or refuse to talk to those who hurt us. Those choices leave the door open for the enemy to work in our life. Instead, we need to use the equipment God's Word has provided for us to hold on to our peace.

Renewing our mind with the truth of God's Word by meditating on it, gravitating towards it and holding on to it with our thoughts and emotions is what brings us stability. When we have this stability, we'll be able to stay calm through life's challenges because we are maintaining our peace in difficult times. We will respond from that place of peace instead of frustration or anxiety.

We've already talked about how important it is that we become a forgiver and choose to release people from any offense we may have had towards them, because if we hold on to unforgiveness, it's going to steal our peace. We've also talked about the value of controlling our emotions, because if they're left unchecked, they can steal our peace, too. And we learned that we have the power of the Holy Spirit on the inside of us to exercise self-control, so when we yield to Him, we can maintain our peace and control our emotions.

In this lesson, we're going to learn how to maintain our peace by recognizing the good in our lives and being thankful. As humans, it's really easy for us to focus on the negatives. Have you ever been around someone who doesn't tell you the good that you do, but they're often complaining to you about your mistakes? They don't encourage you by remembering something you've overcome or an area you've matured in, but they keep pointing out things you still struggle with. This is an easy habit for any of us to fall into, but when we can see the good in ourselves and in others, it brings the power that is available to us to maintain our peace.

Think of a relationship or situation in your life that's frustrating and difficult. Even though it might seem really burdensome, what part of it can you see that is good?

One time Denise met this evangelist who had a conviction in his heart from God to carry a huge, heavy cross on his back across many different countries. He was doing it as unto the Lord to bring people to Him, and God moved through his actions. On a day when he had been carrying the cross for hours and hours, he was exhausted and every muscle in his body hurt. His legs hurt, his feet hurt, his arms hurt. He started to complain, but then he prayed and told God, "Okay, Lord, at least my ears don't hurt." Even though he had a lot to complain about, he decided to focus on the good. When he started thanking God that his ears didn't hurt, it changed his attitude, and he began to thank Him for the other good things in his life.

Just a small decision to start thanking God for one good thing can make a big difference in your thinking and in your ability to maintain your peace in difficult times. First Thessalonians 5:18 says:

> **…In everything give thanks; for this is the will of God in Christ Jesus for you.**

Notice how it doesn't say to thank God *for* everything, but even *in* the bad things we should thank God. When Denise was facing some really difficult symptoms in her body, she chose to thank and praise God in spite of how she felt. When she received prayer, it also made a difference, and she began to feel better. Her choice to thank God opened the door for His healing to flow in her life.

When we just focus on the negative things we feel, all we are doing is complaining, but when we start thanking God in the middle of the problem, we open the door for Heaven to move on our behalf.

Denise loves to call attention to the apostle Paul, because there is so much we can learn from this great man of God. At the time he wrote Philippians, scholars say that Paul was in a horrible prison, surrounded by death and standing in sewage. Can you imagine? And in that small book — just four chapters long — the words *joy* or *rejoicing* appear **19 times**.

How did Paul do it? How did he manage to rejoice, to be an encouragement to all of us two thousand years later, in the middle of circumstances he had every right to complain about? It was the power of God in him through the Holy Spirit. Philippians 4:4 (*KJV*) says to "rejoice in the Lord alway[s]: and again I say, Rejoice!"

Then in verse 6, Paul declared:

> **Be anxious for nothing, but in everything by prayer and supplication, with thanksgiving, let your requests be made known to God.**

Right here we see a huge key to maintaining our peace — thanksgiving.

Many times, when things were not going well in Denise's life, she would focus on thanking God for just one thing at a time — even things that seemed small, such as her bed or her clothes — and as she reflected on each one, her faith and peace were built and she realized how much she had to be thankful for.

The Bible says that every good and perfect gift has come down from above, so every good thing that we have is straight from God (*see* James 1:17). That is why we can be thankful. Anybody can complain, but when we choose to thank God in hard times, we're opening a huge door to experience the kind of peace God has placed in us that bypasses our natural understanding — the kind of peace we can have even when things don't make sense (*see* Philippians 4:7).

Your Thankfulness Makes A Difference For Others

When we focus on the good in our lives, it's easier to be thankful and peaceful. We all have things we can complain about, but it doesn't serve us well. Philippians 2:14 and 15 says:

> **Do all things without complaining and disputing, that you may become blameless and harmless, children of God without fault in the midst of a crooked and perverse generation, among whom you shine as lights in the world.**

When we choose to give thanks instead of complaining in difficult times, we are shining God's light in a dark and perverse world. And when we continue to let His light shine through us, people will notice and maybe even say, "I don't know what you've got, but I want it."

There are so many people around you on a daily basis that don't have peace, and they have no idea how to get it. That is why this principle of maintaining our peace is so important, and one of the best ways to help those around us.

When we let people see the Holy Spirit at work in our hearts, we give them the hope that things can be better. It allows us to point them to

Jesus, the Prince of Peace. In Isaiah 53:5, it says the chastisement of our peace was upon Him. That means Jesus took on everything that could steal your peace when He went to the Cross, so you can have peace in the middle of hard times.

The Power of Perspective

Have you ever known someone that was constantly dissatisfied, even when you do everything you possibly can for them? Is that kind of attitude attractive? Of course not. Do they have peace? Probably not. Are they thankful? Again, probably not. It's impossible to be thankful and complain at the same time.

When we keep meditating on all of the opportunities we have to complain, it's like having an upset stomach. It's a dissatisfaction that keeps you feeling miserable and unhappy and unable to enjoy life and engage with people in a positive way. Even if you've grown past the point of complaining out loud, it's still not pleasant or peaceful to hold on to a complaining attitude on the inside. Yet another reason to choose thankfulness.

On the program, Denise shared a situation many years ago when she and Rick were extremely poor, out of God's will, and trying to feed their family with an empty refrigerator. At the time they just had their first son, Paul, and he was nearly two years old. That empty refrigerator was starting to get to Denise's head, and she felt overwhelmed and started complaining over and over about the empty fridge.

Then she noticed a book called *You Get What You Say*, and thought to herself, *I'm going to read this book*. Eventually she reached a point in the book where the author's refrigerator was also empty. She thought, *Hmm, that sounds familiar*.

Every time he walked by his empty refrigerator, Denise read that he would look at the refrigerator — even though there was no food in it — and he would start praising God.

Denise thought, *Well, I don't have anything to lose. I'm just going to do what he did*. So, every time she walked by their refrigerator, she said, "Praise the Lord! Thank you, Jesus! God, You are so good! Thank you that You provide all of our needs. I worship You, Lord, for what You're doing in my life. Hallelujah!"

After doing this for several days, somebody called them and said, "God has put you on our hearts and we want to go to the grocery store and fill your refrigerator and your cabinets with food." What a testimony!

What did her praise do? It opened the door for God to come and do something in their lives in the area where they had need. What would complaining have done? It would probably have positioned her to stay exactly where she was with no results.

But praising — choosing to thank God and to do all things without grumbling and complaining — causes us, as that verse says, to become blameless children of God who shine without fault in this dark generation.

If there was ever a time that people need to see us shining, it is *now*. People are confused, worried, suicidal, addicted to drugs and alcohol, dealing with divorce and pain of all kinds… and we have the answer. When we can maintain our peace in difficult times, we can share that peace with them.

Denise shared a sweet story to illustrate the ability we have to turn off complaining and turn on thanksgiving. Many years ago, when Rick and Denise's grandson William was about four years old, they took him and his sister to a nice dinner to spend time with them and William was so well-behaved. When Denise thanked him for his behavior, she asked, "How did you do it?" He said, "Well, Grandma, I turned off my disobedient button that was right back here (making a turn-off sound). I turned it off, and I turned on (making a turn-on sound) my obedient button."

Even at his young age, he knew that he had enough willpower to say, "I can turn on my obedience or turn off my obedience." In the same way, we can choose to thank God for every good thing in our lives.

Denise's prayer for you:

> Father, I thank You for my friend and I thank You for the power of the Holy Spirit that's on the inside of us. Thank You that by aligning ourselves with that power, we can choose to be thankful and experience Your peace that comes when we choose not to complain. And because we know this power is from You, we give You all the praise for this, Jesus. We love You, Lord! In Jesus' name, amen.

STUDY QUESTIONS

**Be diligent to present yourself approved to God, a worker
who does not need to be ashamed, rightly dividing the word of truth.
— 2 Timothy 2:15**

1. When and why is it good to be thankful (*see* Psalm 103:1-4, 107:1-3, 118:24, 1 Thessalonians 5:18)? What happens in our hearts and minds when we pray with thanksgiving (*see* Philippians 4:4-7)?

2. Staying thankful isn't always easy, but it's crucial to holding on to peace. What does the Bible say we should do when it's difficult to remain grateful (*see* Hebrews 13:15)?

3. What are some ways we can put this into practice (*see* Isaiah 26:3, Philippians 4:11-13)?

PRACTICAL APPLICATION

**But be doers of the word,
and not hearers only, deceiving yourselves.
— James 1:22**

1. When Denise started thanking God regardless of her empty refrigerator, provision came. What did you think about how her thankfulness opened the door for that to occur?

2. Is there a time in your life that God unmistakably provided for you? What happened?

3. What is one thing you are waiting for Him to provide in this season? Take a minute to tell the Lord what you need, releasing your trust and responsibility to Him, knowing He's watching out for you.

TOPIC

Maintaining Peace by Seeing Your Problem As Smaller Than God!

SCRIPTURES

1. **1 Samuel 17:44-47** — And the Philistine said to David, "Come to me, and I will give your flesh to the birds of the air and the beasts of the field!" Then David said to the Philistine, "You come to me with a sword, with a spear, and with a javelin. But I come to you in the name of the Lord of hosts, the God of the armies of Israel, whom you have defied. This day the Lord will deliver you into my hand, and I will strike you and take your head from you. And this day I will give the carcasses of the camp of the Philistines to the birds of the air and the wild beasts of the earth, that all the earth may know that there is a God in Israel. Then all this assembly shall know that the Lord does not save with sword and spear; for the battle is the Lord's, and He will give you into our hands."

SYNOPSIS

David was a shepherd boy, and when he showed up at the battlefield, he was able to defeat Goliath because he knew God was so much bigger than the problem. After watching Him intervene to help him defeat both a lion and a bear that had attacked his sheep, David knew God was more than able to give him victory over the giant in his way. Because Saul and the army of Israel didn't have a clear view of God's greatness and power, they saw God as too small to defeat Goliath — but because David saw the *problem as smaller* than God — he got to see God's power in action, and he overcame on behalf of all of Israel.

The emphasis of this lesson:

When we have a true view of our problems in relation to our God, it becomes so much easier to trust Him and stay calm in difficult times. Focus on how much bigger God is than your problem, and you will be able to overcome it with peace.

Remember Who Is Greater

One of the most important things to remember about God's Word is that it *never* returns void (*see* Isaiah 55:11). As the Word of God makes its way into your heart, there are seeds that are planted there, and over time, those seeds grow up and produce the fruit of God's Word in your life.

In Rick and Denise's church recently, she had a word of knowledge that God was healing someone and she shared that word with the congregation. Not long after that, she received a testimony from a woman who had been having a physical health problem for four years. She'd been to several doctors that were no help, but when she heard what Denise shared from the Lord, this lady received that for herself and wrote, "I am receiving my healing, and I am already feeling better after four years!"

We should never take the Word of God for granted because it is so powerful. We should never be content to leave it on our bedside table and just look at it occasionally or not pick it up at all, because it carries the very healing power of God — healing power that we need.

Another testimony Denise shared was from a woman who had pancreatic cancer, and she couldn't receive any treatments. She just had to keep going to work, but she made a decision to read the Bible. She read the whole Bible within two months, and despite not having any doctor or medical care, her body healed completely. That's how powerful the Word of God is!

In the first lesson, we began with talking about the importance of forgiveness, because when we have unforgiveness in our heart, it's nearly impossible for us to maintain peace. Then we learned that using self-control to rein in our emotions, being intentionally thankful and focusing on the good in our lives also helps us to cultivate peace.

In today's lesson we're going to focus on how God — the One who is greater than anything and anyone — is on the inside of you. If we want to maintain peace in difficult times, we need to recognize and remember that God is always bigger than our problem.

David Saw God As Bigger Than Goliath

Because David knew God and had seen His faithfulness, he knew he could face the giant Goliath. Some problems that we encounter are not of our own making — they're actually somebody else's problem — but we get pulled into it. That's what happened to David in First Samuel 17 when he fought Goliath. As we go through that chapter, we see that David was not originally the person assigned to face that giant.

It was the responsibility of Saul and the army of Israel to take down the Philistines. As they were facing the huge task set before them, the Israelite army stood on one side of the mountain, and the Philistines stood on the other. Goliath was their champion, and with a valley between them, he came down every day to dare Israel to send out their best fighter to take him on in mortal combat. The army that lost would become the slaves of the army that won. His attitude, his size, his sheer strength, and experience in battle quickly intimidated the entire army of Israel, including Saul — the one they should have been able to look to for courage because he was their leader.

This went on for 40 days.

The Bible says they were dismayed and dreadfully afraid, and fear could have only grown more and more each day. Can you imagine listening to the constant challenges and threats from Goliath, feeling stuck in that position of fear for so long and helpless to do anything about it?

Satan, who is our enemy, comes against us in a very similar way. He brings lies, accusation, condemnation, and judgment to our minds to intimidate us and keep us in fear, anxiety, and torment. Friend, that can't be us. The Bible says we are to resist the devil right away (*see* 1 Peter 5:9 *AMPC*), so it is critically important we recognize his tactics *on the very first day* and resist those thoughts he brings to us. Not on the fortieth day, not on the thirty-fifth day, not on the twentieth day, but on the *first* day. Otherwise, we will stand still in fear like Saul and his army did for far too long.

When the enemy comes with those tormenting thoughts, we must recognize and say to ourselves, "*This is NOT the voice of my Father. This is NOT the voice of my Shepherd. This is the voice of the liar, thief and destroyer who's out to scare me into submission, but I am shutting the door in his face! I don't have to be afraid of him, because my God, who is in me, is greater than my problem and greater than my enemy.*"

Because Saul and his army didn't have that mindset, they didn't see that God was bigger than their problem. They just stood there, frozen and intimidated by the giant.

Then David shows up. He hears Goliath's taunting and sees how fearful the Israelite soldiers are. He asks, "What is the reward for the one who takes down this giant?" They tell him the reward will be great wealth, the king's daughter in marriage, and exemption from taxes for the family of the man who defeats Goliath (*see* 1 Samuel 17:25-27).

David has a totally different perception of the giant than everyone else. He doesn't call him a giant by focusing on his physical size — instead he calls him "this uncircumcised Philistine" (*see* v. 26). "How can this uncircumcised Philistine defy the armies of the living God?" David asks. He sees that God is bigger than the problem, despite the fact that Goliath was nearly nine feet tall. Remember that Saul and his army were responsible... but they weren't taking care of their predicament.

It was David, a little shepherd boy who came down to feed his brothers, who saw the situation as it was — because of his relationship with God, he had more power available to him then an uncircumcised foreigner actively defying the army of the living God.

My God is bigger than that giant, he thought. *That giant is smaller than my God. I'm going to take him down and I'm going to receive that reward.*

That one thought, that simple perspective, was enough to give him the courage to go into battle. Even when Goliath told David he would feed his corpse to the birds and wild animals, David was unmoved. First Samuel 17:44-47 unpacks the beginning of this fatal duel:

> **And the Philistine said to David, "Come to me, and I will give your flesh to the birds of the air and the beasts of the field!" Then David said to the Philistine, "You come to me with a sword, with a spear, and with a javelin. But I come to you in the name of the Lord of hosts, the God of the armies of Israel, whom you have defied. This day the Lord will deliver you into my hand, and I will strike you and take your head from you. And this day I will give the carcasses of the camp of the Philistines to the birds of the air and the wild beasts of the earth, that all the earth may know that there is a God in Israel. Then all this assembly shall know that the Lord does not save with sword and spear; for the battle is the Lord's, and He will give you into our hands."**

Can you sense David's boldness? Right after this incredible exchange, David took his slingshot and launched a rock that hit the giant right in his forehead. Goliath then fell to the ground, and David took the giant's sword from its sheath and cut off his head.

Why did David win the victory? The same reason we can experience victory today: because he "saw" with the eyes of faith. When we see with *those* eyes, we live with an awareness that God is infinitely greater than our problem. As we choose to focus on His Word, we can maintain our peace in difficult times, and see Him intervene on our behalf in a mighty way.

One more thing David did that was very powerful. Before he fought Goliath, he repeated to Saul all the victories that he had experienced as a shepherd boy (*see* vv. 34-37). He remembered how God helped him to overtake a lion and a bear to save his sheep, and he knew Goliath would be just like that lion and bear — that God would give him victory as he sought to protect His people.

Look Back at How God Has Come Through

In the same way, we need to remember the victories that God has brought about in our past. If you're facing a problem right now that feels like a giant, remember what He has already done in your life. What have you been healed of? From what has He set you free? Who did He give you favor with? When did you receive peace in the middle of difficulty? How has He protected you?

Know that the same God who showed up for you in those hard times is the same God who will make a way for you now. The Bible says that God never changes (*see* Malachi 3:6). Even if what you're currently going through feels like the most difficult thing you've ever faced in your life, *there is hope.*

You can have peace in the knowledge that receiving the victory is not about your ability or doing everything right. It's about how great, power-ful, and faithful *He* is. He's promised to never leave you or forsake you (*see* Deuteronomy 31:6) and that very same resurrection power of Christ now lives in you and will empower you for everything you'll walk through (*see* Romans 8:11).

Because David saw something completely different than Saul and his army, he seized the God-sized opportunity for victory that they had been blind to for 40 straight days. A young shepherd boy who saw that God was bigger than their problem was the one who saw Him show up and deliver Israel in a mind-blowing way.

The God whom you love and who loves you — the same God who created the universe — He is bigger than your problem and you can trust in Him. He's not far away somewhere in space, He is *right here with you*. We can face any problem in our lives with the help of His Holy Spirit inside us.

Denise's prayer for you:

> Father, I thank You for everyone who is reading this prayer right now. Lord, we come to You in this moment. We might not be able to see or feel the answer right now, but God, we know that You are the answer. And we proclaim right now today, together, that You are bigger than this problem, You have the answer, and we can trust You. Thank You that we don't have to fear, because Your presence is constantly with us, and You never leave us nor forsake us. Thank You for being our best, most excellent Helper in times of trouble. We love You, Father. We pray this in the name of Jesus. Amen.

STUDY QUESTIONS

Be diligent to present yourself approved to God, a worker who does not need to be ashamed, rightly dividing the word of truth.
— 2 Timothy 2:15

1. Read 1 Samuel 17:34-37; 45-47. What about David's attitude and vision stands out to you the most? What quality did his awareness of God's power and greatness give him in the fight?

2. Our view of God drastically affects our ability to receive from Him, either positively or negatively. What happened when the king's officer questioned the word of the Lord through the prophet Elisha (*see* 2 Kings 7:1-20)? What stands out to you about this story?

3. In contrast, what happened when Abraham saw and believed God's power and love for him (*see* Genesis 15:6, Romans 4:16-22, Hebrews 11:8-12)?

PRACTICAL APPLICATION

**But be doers of the word,
and not hearers only, deceiving yourselves.
— James 1:22**

1. What problem or area of life feels (or has felt) like an insurmountable obstacle — a Goliath?

2. Now, take a look back: What's a smaller victory that God has won for you (like the lion and the bear)? It might be a way He's protected you, provided for you, or sent someone to help you at a time when you really needed it.

3. Take a moment to write out both, then pray and invite God to give you His boldness and power to keep going with the knowledge that He's been faithful before, and He'll be faithful again.

LESSON 5

TOPIC

Maintaining Peace by Knowing the Lover on the Inside

SCRIPTURES

1. **Galatians 5:22,23** — But the fruit of the Spirit is love, joy, peace, longsuffering, kindness, goodness, faithfulness, gentleness, self-control. Against such there is no law.

2. **Mark 4:35** — On the same day, when evening had come, He said to them, "Let us cross over to the other side."

3. **Mark 4:38,39** — But He was in the stern, asleep on a pillow. And they awoke Him and said to Him, "Teacher, do You not care that we are perishing?" Then He arose and rebuked the wind, and said to the sea, "Peace, be still!" And the wind ceased and there was a great calm.

4. **1 Corinthians 6:19** — Or do you not know that your body is the temple of the Holy Spirit who is in you, whom you have from God, and you are not your own?

5. **Romans 6:17,18** — But God be thanked that though you were slaves of sin, yet you obeyed from the heart that form of doctrine to which you were delivered. And having been set free from sin, you became slaves of righteousness.

6. **Colossians 1:13,14** — He has delivered us from the power of darkness and conveyed us into the kingdom of the Son of His love, in whom we have redemption through His blood, the forgiveness of sins.

7. **2 Corinthians 13:5** — ...Do you not know yourselves, that Jesus Christ is in you?....

SYNOPSIS

Did you know that the Holy Spirit — who is the representation of Jesus on the earth — lives in you? Because He is in you, you have all the characteristics of who He is on the inside of you, including love, joy, and peace in the middle of chaotic situations. Just like Jesus in the boat with His disciples during a storm, knowing His love will strengthen and empower you to rest in God's protection, remain calm, and take authority over the enemy's attacks.

The emphasis of this lesson:

The Holy Spirit is the third member of the Trinity, and He's the lover on the inside of you. In every moment, He's present with you, encouraging your heart, healing your soul, bringing forth the fruit of God's character, and interceding on your behalf.

You Have Peace on the Inside of You

Throughout the first four lessons, we've talked about how important it is to forgive instead of holding on to bitterness, manage our emotions to exercise self-control, keep our focus on the positives and praise God in the middle of our challenges. And then in the last lesson, we learned the power of seeing God as bigger than our problem and our problem as smaller than God.

In today's lesson, we're going to focus on the joy of knowing and experiencing the Holy Spirit as the lover on the inside of you. We want to know everything we can about Him, because He's the One who is going to help us maintain peace in difficult times.

When you were born again, the presence and power of the Holy Spirit came into you. With Him came the nine fruits of the Spirit in Galatians 5:22 and 23, which begin with love, joy, and peace. The verses go on to add:

...longsuffering, kindness, goodness, faithfulness, gentleness, self-control; against such there is no law.

Did you ever notice that the third fruit mentioned here is *peace*? This means that God's peace is inside us, in our spirit. Even if we don't feel that peace right now, it is in us through the Holy Spirit. It's not something that we work for or pray numerous times about, it's a free gift given to us when we are born again — we just need to become acquainted with that aspect of the Holy Spirit, which is His peace.

Imagine if you knew a genuinely amazing person you were free to do daily life with, and every day you saw something new that made you appreciate them more. You were able to witness their patience with a slower cashier at the store, how kind they were to a coworker having a hard time, how gentle they were with a child selling cookies for their school fundraiser. Then you saw how they exercised self-control in a frustrating situation that would have made the average person lash out, and it dawns on you, *This is the most peaceful person I've ever met.*

Do you know that inside you are all of those attributes? The kindness, the patience, the gentleness, the self-control...the *peace* of God is on the inside of you by the mighty and wonderful Holy Spirit.

Calm in the Middle of the Storm

The peace of God is not what the world calls peace — His peace isn't based on any circumstances that we face. It's a conquering peace that comes from within — it's powerful and can even stop storms. If you're wondering, *What? His peace can stop the storms in my life?* It's true! In Mark 4:35, we see how the peace of Jesus calmed a storm as He was in the middle of a lake with His disciples:

... "Let us cross over to the other side."

When Jesus says something, He means it. He wasn't thinking, *Well, maybe we'll cross over to the other side.* No, He said, in essence, "Hey guys, *let us cross over* to the other side. *We are going* to the other side." Jesus was so peaceful, maybe even tired, and He fell into a deep sleep in the boat.

As Jesus was sleeping, a terrible storm came and the boat became unsteady. In the middle of howling winds and overwhelming waves, the disciples could tell that this was a life-threatening storm. Yet He was sleeping peacefully in the middle of it, not worried at all.

Denise used to think that He must have been in a special part of the boat where there wasn't any water, because the water had to have been rising in the boat. That's why the disciples feared for their lives — they were afraid the boat would go down, and that they would sink with it.

When the water was coming up around Jesus, He was right there with them. The water was rising around Him, too, yet He was still sleeping and at peace. Is that not magnificent? That kind of peace is conquering peace.

The peace that Jesus was living in is the same peace that He gave you. He was not moved by the storm, the howling winds, or the water rising around Him. That is amazing peace.

You Can Rest in God's Protection

Denise shared this story with a young woman, and she told Denise that her neighbors were so loud that the noise was stealing her sleep. She couldn't do anything about it and was frustrated. Later, she wrote Denise and said, "I listened to what you said about how Jesus was asleep even though the water was rising up around Him, but He was still asleep in peace. I decided that if God had that kind of peace on the inside of me, that I was going to sleep. I slept all night and my neighbors didn't bother me at all."

Did the neighbors change? No, but *she* changed. She recognized the peace that passes all understanding was on the inside of her through the Holy Spirit and she let that peace rule in her heart instead of worry.

Continuing on with the story in Mark 4:38 and 39, it says that Jesus was in the stern of the ship asleep on a pillow...

> **...And they** [the disciples] **awoke Him and said to Him, "Teacher, do You not care that we are perishing?" Then He arose and rebuked the wind, and said to the sea, "Peace, be still!" And the wind ceased and there was a great calm.**

The peace that Jesus spoke out of, is the very same peace He's given you in your spirit, because He loves you so much. He's the lover of our soul who lives in us and the One who helps us hold on to our peace in hard times. First Corinthians 6:19 says:

> **Or do you not know that your body is the** [very] **temple of the Holy Spirit who is in you, whom you have from God, and you are not your own?**

So, the Holy Spirit lives in you, which means your body is His home. Romans 6:17 and 18 also tells us:

> **But God be thanked that though you were slaves of sin, yet you obeyed from the heart that form of doctrine to which you were delivered. And having been set free from sin, you became slaves of righteousness.**

When Jesus came into our heart through the Holy Spirit, the Bible says that He *redeemed* us. There's so much love in that word, *redeemed*. In the Greek language, *redeemed* is the word *exagorazó*, and it comes from a place not far from where the apostle Paul was living at the time — the Agora.

In the Agora, slaves were put on display and up for sale, so the place was filled with current slave owners and others who wanted to purchase slaves. Potential buyers would look at each one, open their mouth and check their teeth, even slap them in the face and punch or kick them to see how much pain they could withstand. They wanted to find out if a slave was strong enough and if their spirit was broken enough to do whatever they wanted.

That sounds a lot like the devil, doesn't it? He always comes with abuse, trying to put us down, steal from us, and destroy our joy, liberty, and life. Scripture says we used to be essentially owned by the devil, because we were slaves of sin (*see* Romans 6:20).

But then came another kind of person — a redeemer. The word *exagorazó* is the term for when a slave was bought out of that life by a redeemer — where the price was paid for their freedom. He would say, "You don't have to remain in this state — I am going to purchase you from your owner, out of that terrible slavery. And then I am setting you free."

That's exactly what Jesus did for us. He freed us from the slavery of sin. He came in with His great love and power and said, "I love you so much that I am bringing you out of this slavery that's been destroying you — with the price of my Blood you are free from this moment on."

The Bible says in Colossians 1:13 and 14 that God redeemed us out of darkness and transferred us into the kingdom of His dear Son. That's what Jesus did for you by the Holy Spirit; do you see how deeply He loves you? If we're going to make it through these difficult times, one of the most important things to remember is that we were bought out of slavery, so we have no connection or obligation to the old way of life — we can live totally new and free because of His love for us!

When you were born again, the Holy Spirit came into you and gave you the very love of God and the same power of the resurrection (*see* Romans 5:5, 8:11). In Second Corinthians 13:5, it asks:

> **... Do you not know yourselves that Jesus Christ is in you? ...**

Friend, Jesus is truly the lover on the inside of you — the One who will never abandon you. Because He bought you out of slavery, you are no longer your own. You were bought with the price of His Blood when you were delivered out of that bondage and welcomed into His kingdom of light.

Even when we don't feel Him at work in us, we can know He is working out a plan of salvation on our behalf that is truly magnificent. It takes time, but He will complete it (*see* Philippians 1:6). He is saving us, delivering us, and setting us free from fear by giving us His peace and soundness of mind. That is what He is doing on the inside of us. When we recognize His power, that we are not our own, and that we belong to Him, it becomes much easier to know and remember He is watching out for us in every moment, and we are never alone.

Remember this verse that we mentioned earlier, in First Corinthians 6:19, it says:

> **Or do you not know that your body is the temple of the Holy Spirit who is in you, whom you have from God, and you are not your own?**

Because Jesus purchased us with His own precious blood, we are free indeed (*see* John 8:36). We are not slaves to sin anymore, in any way, but free to live in righteousness. He brought us out of slavery, and He placed us in His kingdom. We are not our own, we are His. He has set us free from slavery to the enemy and every kind of bondage imaginable.

Denise's prayer for you:

Father, I thank You for the Word of God that tells us the truth. It reminds us that we don't belong to this world, its habits, curses, sin, and deception. But we belong to You, and the Holy Spirit is the lover on the inside of us. Lord, thank You that You want us to maintain peace in these difficult times and get to know You in a new and precious way. We pray these things in the wonderful and powerful name of Jesus. Amen.

STUDY QUESTIONS

**Be diligent to present yourself approved to God, a worker
who does not need to be ashamed, rightly dividing the word of truth.
— 2 Timothy 2:15**

1. Knowing that the Lover on the inside of you is with you and for you is critically important. What does God's Word say about His presence in you (*see* Matthew 1:23; John 14:20; 2 Timothy 4:17; 1 John 4:4,16)?
2. What did the Holy Spirit enable Jesus to do (*see* Isaiah 11:1-5, Romans 8:10-11)? What does His presence in you enable you to do (*see* John 14:26; 15:4-5; 16:13; Acts 1:8)?

PRACTICAL APPLICATION

**But be doers of the word,
and not hearers only, deceiving yourselves.
— James 1:22**

1. When you think of the Holy Spirit as a lover on the inside of you, what kind of picture does that create in your mind? Are you experiencing Him as a positive, comforting presence? If not, ask Him to show you what it truly means to let Him love you — He's always ready and waiting to love, comfort, and strengthen you.
2. What do you think you might do differently if you remembered that God is literally *always* with you? Would you be less afraid? Have more boldness? Be ready to share His love with more people and pursue the dreams He's placed in your heart? Ask Him to give you a greater awareness of His closeness and power, and you'll begin to see His intervention in so many ways.

TOPIC

Maintaining Peace by Knowing the Comforter

SCRIPTURES

1. **John 14:16** — And I will pray the Father, and He will give you another Helper, that He may abide with you forever.

2. **Romans 8:26** — Likewise the Spirit also helps in our weaknesses. For we do not know what we should pray for as we ought, but the Spirit Himself makes intercession for us with groanings which cannot be uttered.

3. **2 Corinthians 13:5** — ... Do you not know yourselves, that Jesus Christ is in you?

SYNOPSIS

The Holy Spirit is the greatest Helper you could ever imagine. When you're hurting, He's your comforter. When you're lost, He's your guide. When you're lacking, He's your provider. When you get off track, He gently nudges you in the right direction. When you learn to embrace His presence, you'll find His help in every area of your life, no matter how big or small.

The emphasis of this lesson:

The greatest Comforter that we could ever ask for or imagine is present in the person of the Holy Spirit. In every moment, He's ready, able, and willing to order your steps, touch your heart, and bring peace to your soul.

You Have a Comforter

So far, we've learned about the power of forgiveness, focusing on the good in our lives, managing our emotions, and recognizing the power of the Holy Spirit inside us to exercise self-control. Jesus has given us everything we need to live a godly life and be a witness of His love on this earth — that is

His will, and His Word is filled with so many things to help us maintain our peace in difficult times.

In this lesson, we will learn more about the Holy Spirit. We've talked about His peace inside us, but it is also important to know more about Him as a *person* — His attributes, personality, and reputation. We can see these things very clearly when Jesus talked about the Holy Spirit in John 14:16, saying:

> **And I will pray the Father, and He will give you another Helper, that He may abide with you forever.**

This is so comforting! That phrase in the Greek language means *another helper who is just like Me*, so Jesus was basically saying, "I'm going to go away, but I'm going to send you another Helper. In the same way that I helped and comforted you in this journey for the last three years, the Holy Spirit will come to help and comfort you, so you will never be alone."

What an amazing attribute of the Holy Spirit — our Helper. Even in our weaknesses we are not disqualified because He comes to help us. We may criticize ourselves for our shortcomings, but He never does; He comes to help.

You Have a Helper

The Holy Spirit always wants us to experience victory, so when we get into a difficult situation and want to maintain our peace, we can always pray this simple prayer: "Help me, Holy Spirit." In Romans 8:26, the apostle Paul wrote:

> **Likewise the Spirit also helps in our weaknesses. For we do not know what we should pray for as we ought, but the Spirit Himself makes intercession for us with groanings which cannot be uttered.**

There again we see that word *help*, which in the Greek is called *sunantilambanomai*. It's a long Greek word that's only been used in the Bible ONE time. Let's break down this word into a few smaller pieces so we can understand it more easily.

The first part is *sun*, which means He's *coming alongside of you*. He is *right there* when you encounter a situation where you need peace.

The next part is *anti*, which means *against*, and this word carries within it a sense of attitude. So, when something comes against you, the Holy Spirit inside you has an *attitude against* that thing that's trying to bring you down.

Next, *lambano* means that He's going to *take it*, in the same way that a thief would *grab* a purse or valuable item someone was carrying down the street.

Putting all of this together, we understand that the Holy Spirit is our Helper; He is right next to us, He has an attitude against anything that tries to bring us down, and He is ready to take it away from us. He is going to take away that thing that is trying to bring you down to bring you back to a place of peace.

What a Helper! Even a short, heartfelt prayer of, "Holy Spirit, help me," opens the door for Him to intervene in so many powerful ways. When we cry out to Him, He comes immediately to help.

You Have a Guide

Another one of his attributes is that He is the Spirit of Truth. You can always trust whatever He says to you, because He's guiding you into all truth (*see* John 16:13). Not long ago, He was speaking the truth to Denise, encouraging and reminding her to do what she said she would do. He will nudge and speak to us gently, always helping us to develop good character, and one attribute of that is to keep our word.

Many, many years ago, the Holy Spirit was guiding Denise about where to go to college, but she was fighting Him. She didn't want to go to the college that God wanted her to go to, so she went to the one she had always dreamed of going to instead.

When she got there, she was absolutely miserable, crying herself to sleep every single night. She loved God, but felt torn because she was out of His will. If people had looked at her life from the outside, they could have thought, "Oh, she's singing here and there, God is blessing her, she's a Christian girl in a Christian college, she must be so happy." Yet, she was out of God's will and was definitely unhappy. She was supposed to go there again her sophomore year, and even had the money and plans set in place. But the Holy Spirit was so kind and kept nudging her in the right direction.

He eventually told her, "Denise, you can stay at this college and because you're My child I will bless you. But you will never know what it was I wanted to show you."

When she heard this, she repented to the Lord, and made the decision to obey Him. When she told her parents, her dad wasn't happy about it at first, but eventually God changed his heart. When she transferred to the university the Lord directed her to, she had just enough money for her first month to go, but then God made a way for her entire first year to be paid! He guided her in every part of her new college experience, and even showed her who her voice teacher was supposed to be and what her schedule was meant to look like.

If she hadn't heard and followed the gentle, guiding voice of the Holy Spirit, she would never have met Rick, and she would have missed out on her three sons, eight wonderful grandchildren, and the joy of serving the Russian people for over three decades.

That's how important it is to remain sensitive to the One who is in us — He is always guiding us to what is best for us, which is God's perfect will. You are His, so He will not lead you the wrong way. He will guide you. That is quite a lover, and that's what He will do for you.

The Holy Spirit is so wonderful — He is literally God on the inside of you, and He is just like Jesus. The apostle Paul said in 2 Corinthians 13:5:

...Do you not know...that Jesus Christ [lives] in you?

Friend, He has deposited so much on the inside of us. That is why we should listen to Him, because He only has good things in store. If He is telling you to do something, and you don't want to, do it anyway. He's not trying to frustrate you; He's working to bless you. He's not trying to diminish your life; He's working to help you get to your best life.

Have you ever sensed the Holy Spirit communicate things such as:

- *Don't go there; try here instead.*
- *Don't eat that; you'll regret it.*
- *Don't say that; it could do more damage than you realize.*

He's not telling you those things because He's trying to keep you from having a good time — He's telling you those things because He's trying to protect you. He's going to push you right through to victory in whatever it is you are dealing with if you'll listen to Him.

Is He dealing with your heart about something right now? Maybe He's told you to start a business and you've been too afraid. Maybe He has gently nudged you about an area in your life that needs to change and you feel like you can't do it…but you can. The Holy Spirit is right there to help you; to be your best friend, and your guide into all truth. Lean on Him and watch Him transform your life.

Denise's prayer for you:

> Father, we pray together right now in the name of Jesus, and I recognize the power of the Holy Spirit touching my friends who are reading this. We surrender to You, Holy Spirit, to do the will of God for our lives. You desire to help us, lead us, and guide us so that we can maintain our peace in difficult times, and we give You all the praise. Thank You, Jesus, for giving us the Holy Spirit — He's just like You! You're amazing, we love You, and it's in Your name we pray. Amen.

STUDY QUESTIONS

Be diligent to present yourself approved to God, a worker who does not need to be ashamed, rightly dividing the word of truth.
— 2 Timothy 2:15

1. Think about the Holy Spirit as our Comforter; why do you think He provides comfort for those He loves (*see* 2 Corinthians 1:3,4)?
2. What will it be like when Jesus comes in His glory at the end of time (*see* Revelation 21:1-7)? How does it make you feel to read this passage? What do you look forward to most when He comes back?

PRACTICAL APPLICATION

But be doers of the word,
and not hearers only, deceiving yourselves.
—James 1:22

1. Think back for a moment to Denise's story about being in college. Have you ever been out of God's will before? How did you realize it and respond?

2. When we received Jesus as our Lord and Savior, the Holy Spirit came into us at that moment. Because He is our Helper, where do you need His gentle guidance right now?

3. How does His instruction in our lives show us in what way we should help lead others?

4. The Holy Spirit is the ultimate Comforter — better than any other person, substance, or experience. Which area of life has left you with an ache or sadness? Invite Him to comfort you there, and write out what He whispers to your heart.

TOPIC
Maintaining Peace by Refusing the Trap of Isolation

SCRIPTURES

1. **1 Corinthians 10:13** — No temptation has overtaken you except such as is common to man....

2. **Hebrews 4:14,15** — Seeing then that we have a great High Priest who has passed through the heavens, Jesus the Son of God, let us hold fast our confession. For we do not have a High Priest who cannot sympathize with our weaknesses, but was in all points tempted as we are, yet without sin.

3. **Hebrews 2:18** — For in that He Himself has suffered, being tempted, He is able to aid those who are tempted.

4. **Psalm 139:11,12** — If I say, "Surely the darkness shall fall on me," Even the night shall be light about me; Indeed, the darkness shall not hide from You, but the night shines as the day; the darkness and the light are both alike to You.

5. **James 5:16** — Confess your trespasses to one another, and pray for one another, that you may be healed. The effective, fervent prayer of a righteous man avails much.

SYNOPSIS

What if a few godly friends could make a huge difference in helping you maintain peace? When you have believers in your life who can walk with you through challenging seasons, listen to you when you need to pour your heart out, encourage you with truth from God's Word, and spur you on to make healthy choices, you are beyond blessed.

The emphasis of this lesson:

One of the most underrated ways to maintain peace is through finding and cultivating relationships with other healthy believers. When you confess your struggles, temptations, and pain to others, you'll be able to experience healing.

You're Never Alone in Any Struggle

In this lesson, we're going to unpack another important aspect of maintaining our peace in difficult times, and that is refusing to isolate ourselves from other people. Like a human body, the Body of Christ is designed as one body with many parts that are all joined together.

In the same way that a body part separated from the main body brings death to it, separation or isolation from the rest of the Body of Christ causes us to experience death in a spiritual context. It is a trap from the enemy that can lead you to a dark place and will definitely steal your peace.

So, what *is* the trap of isolation? It is when we decide to pull away from other believers, even in a small measure. Oftentimes this decision can be driven by pride, embarrassment over a struggle, a prolonged state of deep-seated sadness, or even the fear that nobody will understand what we're going through. Regardless of the cause, isolation is a trap from the enemy and it keeps us from sharing our struggles and receiving healing from the pain that we're going through.

God did not call us to walk alone (*see* Hebrews 10:24,25). So, when we hide our battles and keep tormenting thoughts all to ourselves, that does not protect us, but the exact opposite is true. There is no safety in the darkness; that darkness will only increase. And that place of peace seems much farther away because of the darkness in that trap of isolation.

Traps are designed to capture us and keep us bound in the enemy's lies so we cannot escape. He always comes to steal the joy, peace, and fulfillment of walking on the path God has called us to. Just as a physical trap is designed, set and hidden in the forest to trap a wild animal, the enemy's spiritual traps don't say, "Hey! Here I am! I'm a trap!! I'm going to get you!"

No, traps are deceptive; traps are meant to be hidden and quietly bring their victims' demise. The devil has a way of seeming so very logical and rational that it can be incredibly easy to fall for his lies. One negative thought, feeling, fear, or embarrassment at a time, he'll convince us, "Nobody will understand me…and I can't tell anyone." The truth is, there *are* other believers who will understand how you feel. In 1 Corinthians 10:13, it says:

> **No temptation has overtaken you except such as is common to man….**

Notice that word, *common*? That means the same temptation that comes against you also comes against your neighbor, your friend, your spouse, your child. We all go through temptations that are similar, even though they may come to each of us in different forms. Not all of us are tempted to drink alcohol, rob a bank, or shoot someone, but the same spirit is behind every kind of temptation, trying to convince us that we're a special case and that no one will understand. The truth is, no temptation is so unique that no one else has experienced it. And even when you struggle to find another person who's gone through the exact same challenge, you can know that Jesus fully and completely understands what you are going through. The Bible says in Hebrews 4:14 and 15:

> **Seeing then that we have a great High Priest who has passed through the heavens, Jesus the Son of God, let us hold fast our confession. For we do not have a High Priest who cannot sympathize with our weaknesses, but was in all points tempted as we are, yet without sin.**

So, when the devil says, "Nobody will understand your situation or temptation," you can go back to these verses and know that first, all temptation is common to man, and second, Jesus was tempted in exactly the same way that you are, yet He didn't sin. He can truly empathize with us. Hebrews 2:18 says:

> **For in that He Himself has suffered, being tempted, He is able to aid those who are tempted.**

When something is tempting you, trying to steal your peace, and you feel embarrassed and want to crawl into that trap of isolation, *go to Jesus*. He truly understands and has exactly what you need to resist temptation and stay out of the darkness. In Psalm 139:11 and 12, it says:

> **If I say, "Surely the darkness shall fall on me," Even the night shall be light about me; Indeed, the darkness shall not hide from You, but the night shines as the day; the darkness and the light are both alike to You.**

Praise God that no one reading this is in such a dark place that the Lord can't help you! Jesus' perfect, holy sacrifice on the Cross set us free; just call out to Him and let His light shine on your situation.

We All Need a Friend

Many years ago, when Rick and Denise first moved to the former Soviet Union, there was much excitement in front of them. Their three sons were ages three, six, and eight, and they were all on the adventure of a lifetime. It was great, but Denise realized something not long after the move — she needed a friend. She needed somebody she could really talk to and share her heart with, because it was essential for Rick to focus on the ministry and he didn't have as much time as he did before.

At first, Denise believed the lie that no one would understand her problem and that she would have to work it out by herself. That trap of isolation was very dark, and because her insecurities kept her from letting anyone know how she was struggling, she kept going around and around in her mind, trying to find the solution but feeling more like a hamster just spinning on its wheel.

That's exactly what those kinds of thoughts do — you go around and around, yet never arrive at an answer. The real solution is found in James 5:16, which says:

Confess your trespasses to one another, and pray for one another, that you may be healed. The effective, fervent prayer of a righteous man avails much.

Denise read that verse and for the first time, she saw it. She finally told herself, *Denise, you can't do this anymore — you've got to tell someone what you are feeling.*

When you're silently dealing with trials on your own, it feels like a tsunami of emotions, but when you open the door and talk to someone you trust, you bring light into that darkness and the problem begins to lose its power and intensity. As we confess our faults, trespasses, and needs and pray for one another, healing will come. That is our answer.

Thankfully, that is what Denise finally did — she found a friend, opened her heart, and started sharing what she was going through. As the light began coming into her soul, she began to realize that her problem had gotten worse because it had been in the dark, but now that it was in the light, she could find freedom and support.

Maybe you're in a dark place, and you haven't felt confident enough to share a challenge you've been going through. Maybe you've been too embarrassed about different things going on in your life, and you don't know how to tell anyone.

The good news is, no problem or hurt you might be hiding is too dark for Jesus. That verse we read says even in your darkness, there can be light. Even when you are in your darkest place and think there's no hope, wondering, *How in the world am I ever going to get out of this,* He's working in you to bring about His perfect will.

God's Word Is Our Light

Don't you love the Word of God? The Bible says it is a light in the darkness to show us the way. Have you ever been in the dark and then someone turned on a flashlight, and suddenly you saw the way? That's the way it is with the Word of God. He wants to help us avoid and escape the trap of isolation, by confessing our hurts and struggles to each other so we can be healed. That's the promise of James 5, and the Word of God does not lie, so we can depend on that promise.

Denise's prayer for you:

Father, I thank You for the power of Your Word. Your Word says that we will know the truth and the truth will set us free, so we thank You for the truth that we've heard today. And Father, I just lift up my friends reading this right now, that they will take hold of courage and refuse the lies of the devil that say they have to hold everything in. Help us to be a connected Body of Christ and confess our faults one to another and pray for one another, so we may be healed (*see* James 5:16). Lord, I thank You for the power of Your Word that comes to shine on any darkness and set us free. I pray this in Jesus' name, amen.

STUDY QUESTIONS

**Be diligent to present yourself approved to God, a worker
who does not need to be ashamed, rightly dividing the word of truth.
— 2 Timothy 2:15**

1. What does God say will happen for us when we live together in community? How does staying close to other believers make a difference in our everyday lives (*see* Proverbs 27:17; Matthew 18:20; Romans 12:5; Galatians 6:2; Hebrews 10:24,25; 1 John 1:7)?

2. Like James 5:16 says, when we confess things in healthy relationships with other believers who will lovingly encourage us towards growth, we're able to experience healing. In your own words, how did this unfold in Mark 2:1-12?

3. On the other hand, when you see someone who's reluctant in their faith or wandering away from truth, how does Scripture say we should help them get back on track (*see* Galatians 6:1,2)?

PRACTICAL APPLICATION

**But be doers of the word,
and not hearers only, deceiving yourselves.
— James 1:22**

1. Are you currently, or have you ever been, in a situation where you are silently hurting over something you thought you could overcome

alone? Has it ever negatively affected your relationship with God? Did you ever reach out to someone for help?

2. If not, take a minute to bring it into the light with God and ask Him to show you who you can trust and share that with. Pray for the right timing and connect with that person. The grace and healing you'll encounter will change your life in ways you may not have realized.

LESSON 8

TOPIC

Maintaining Peace by Making a Habit of Rejoicing

SCRIPTURES

1. **James 1:1-3** — James, a bondservant of God and of the Lord Jesus Christ, to the twelve tribes which are scattered abroad: Greetings. My brethren, count it all joy when you fall into various trials, knowing that the testing of your faith produces patience.

2. **Philippians 4:4** — Rejoice in the Lord always. Again I will say, rejoice!

3. **Acts 16:25,26** — But at midnight Paul and Silas were praying and singing hymns to God, and the prisoners were listening to them. Suddenly there was a great earthquake, so that the foundations of the prison were shaken; and immediately all the doors were opened and everyone's chains were loosed.

SYNOPSIS

Did you know there is a special kind of joy that can only come under pressure? Like Paul and Silas in prison, we all have an opportunity in the middle of trials to grow closer to God, to impact people around us, and receive power and strength through tough times.

The emphasis of this lesson:

There's a powerful kind of joy that comes when we choose to rejoice and praise God in the middle of challenging circumstances. When we do

this in the face of difficulty, God empowers us to make a huge difference for His glory.

Choosing Joy Cultivates Peace

We've talked about so many ways to maintain peace in difficult times, and an often underrated one is simply *choosing joy*. One of the most powerful attributes that we have on the inside of us by the Holy Spirit is joy. You might be thinking, *I don't have any joy — I don't feel happy.*

Well, the good news is, even when you don't feel happy, joy is still present. Joy is deeper than a feeling because it's one of the fruits of the Spirit, and it is in you. When you agree with that and lean into His presence, it brings joy and helps you stay in that stable and overcoming place of peace like nothing else.

Jesus' half-brother, James — who pastored the church at Jerusalem — understood this principle well. He opened his letter in James 1:1 by introducing himself as:

James, a bondservant of God and of the Lord Jesus Christ...

In their original language, he is actually stating that he's a bondservant of God, *who is* the Lord Jesus Christ. He alone was worthy to give His perfect, holy blood to wipe away our sins, sicknesses, worries, shame, and condemnation (*see* Hebrews 12:24). He and only He is worthy to be praised.

James went on to say in the rest of verse 1 and 2:

To the twelve tribes which are scattered abroad: Greetings. My brethren, count it all joy when you fall into various trials...

James was writing to these believers as they were actively going through trials and hard times. How was he able to say "count it all joy"? Because he was having to do the very same thing. The temptations, trials, and difficulties all of them were fighting — he was facing the very same problems and chose to count it joy.

When James calls them *brethren*, he's purposely putting himself on the same level as them. Although he was Jesus' half-brother — like Jesus, he walked in humility — and encouraged the other believers from a perspective of unity and like-mindedness.

Choosing Joy Brings Power

So, what does it mean to count it all joy in various trials? Well, this kind of joy that James was talking about comes forth in times of testing. This particular kind of joy is interruptive and crushing to the work the enemy is trying to do to defeat you. It might seem counterintuitive, but this type of joy is meant to match the adversity; almost like bread and butter, coffee and cream, or tea and honey. In Russia, people have borscht or meat dumplings known as pelmeni, but they always have it with sour cream, because they go together. So, you see, friend, you can hold on to joy because this kind only comes forth when you are under pressure from a trial.

James' congregation were very likely asking themselves, *How are we going to get joy from these trials?* James knew something they didn't know, or maybe something they had forgotten. In verse three he declared:

Knowing that the testing of your faith produces patience.

James was saying, "In your trial, test, or difficulty, know that this situation is producing power and patience in you." And what kind of power do these hard times produce in us? They're producing in us a *hang-in-there* power, an *I-refuse-to-give-up* type of power.

Create the Habit of Rejoicing

There is a mighty power of joy that is operating through the Holy Spirit in us, and it is a huge weapon that we have against the pressure of the circumstance that's trying to come against us. So, when we choose to be joyful in the midst of a test or a trial, we are opening the door to God's power. In Philippians 4:4, from a filthy prison cell, Paul echoed James when he wrote:

Rejoice in the Lord always. Again I will say, rejoice!

In some commentaries, the word *rejoice* here means to be *habitual* in your rejoicing. What are some things that we habitually do? We are not talking about an external habit like brushing our teeth or going to bed at a certain time; instead, we are talking about the internal habit of how we automatically respond to circumstances.

Often our first reaction to someone's words is to think things such as,

- *I can't believe they said that!*
- *I must not be good enough.*
- *I could never....*
- *This just isn't going to work.*
- *This relationship is falling apart.*

Many times, these triggers and responses have become such an ingrained habit that even if others don't give us a reason to think these things, we have a preprogrammed defense mechanism which systematically tells us, *I've got to protect myself.*

Denise knows one woman who said that when people say certain things, she habitually starts comparing herself to others and feels inferior to them. Sometimes even if nothing is going wrong, she starts putting herself down...because it has become a habit. Habits are powerful tools.

That is why in the Scriptures, the Holy Spirit teaches us to develop the habit of rejoicing — and when we do, we open the door for the power in God's Word to restore our mind to His ways of thinking and bring life to our soul.

Denise used to have an introverted, contemplative type of personality, so when something good happened in her life, instead of rejoicing about it, she would start to wonder, *Oh, what's going to happen now? What bomb is about to drop?* Yet when she began studying these truths, she repented and said to God, "Lord, I recognize my habit, and it's not a good one. Instead of having a fearful mindset, I am going to start rejoicing and trusting You."

As a result, the types of problems that she would previously get upset about didn't seem so huge after all. Now she rejoices in the Lord when she sees even one good thing happening. That is freedom and truth based on God's Word. That is a description of what Jesus was talking about when He said the truth will set us free (*see* John 8:31,32)!

When you choose to rejoice rather than give up, you are generating joy-filled power on the inside of you — that *hang-in-there* power. Instead of getting knocked over by the storms of life, you will be like a palm tree that stays rooted despite devastating hurricane winds (*see* Psalm 92:12,13). Because of your courage, that enduring power that has been developed in you, you will be able to stand strong, be bold, and hold on to your peace, even in difficult times.

Both Silas and the apostle Paul knew what it took to develop this kind of strength in Acts chapter 16. A slave girl who was demon-possessed had been telling fortunes and making a lot of money for her owners; she was set free when Paul commanded that spirit to depart from her in the name of Jesus. When her owners discovered she could no longer make money for them, they were furious. They had Paul and Silas beaten, then threw them into a horrible dungeon.

Needless to say, they were suffering terribly. Their bodies were full of wounds, they were bound in the stocks by the jailer, and they were sitting in darkness. Yet, Acts 16:25 and 26, says:

> **But at midnight Paul and Silas were praying and singing hymns to God, and the prisoners were listening to them. Suddenly there was a great earthquake, so that the foundations of the prison were shaken; and immediately all the doors were opened and everyone's chains were loosed.**

That is the potential of recognizing the power of joy on the inside of you through the Holy Spirit! It was so powerful to that situation that God brought an earthquake to free them and everyone else in the prison. The jailer would have been killed if they all escaped, so he drew his own sword, intending to commit suicide. But Paul and Silas stopped him and said all were still there — no one left the jail. He took Paul and Silas to his home, treated their wounds, and he and his whole family received Jesus (vv. 27-34). That is the power of joy; it turns entire situations around for good.

When we choose to focus on joy, and not on circumstances, we are activating the switch to receive the empowering presence of the Holy Spirit to not give up, and that power goes to work in us. The third person of the Godhead is grabbing hold of that problem we are dealing with and bringing it into subjection for us to overcome in our current situation. What a wonderful God we serve!

Denise's prayer for you:

Father, I thank You for my friends that are reading this right now, and I thank You for the power of the Holy Spirit on the inside of them, that power of joy. As we recognize that power and start rejoicing, Your great power on the inside of us generates that enduring power to press through and remain in peace. We thank You for this mighty power of joy inside us to help us maintain peace in difficult situations. We pray this in the name of our Lord Jesus Christ. Amen.

STUDY QUESTIONS

Be diligent to present yourself approved to God, a worker who does not need to be ashamed, rightly dividing the word of truth.
— 2 Timothy 2:15

1. Read Nehemiah 8:9,10. What about Nehemiah's words to Israel catches your attention?

2. Take another look at Acts 16, reading verses 22 through 34. What happened just before Paul and Silas found themselves in prison? Whose life was totally changed because they chose to rejoice in the middle of an incredibly hard situation? How do you think your decision to rejoice can affect those around you?

PRACTICAL APPLICATION

But be doers of the word,
and not hearers only, deceiving yourselves.
— James 1:22

1. Rejoicing in the middle of a trial is one of our most difficult tasks, but one of the best ways to tap into the strength God wants to give us. What is one trial that has been difficult to see past? Reflecting on what you have learned in this lesson, is there anything you could do or would have done differently?

2. Take a moment to think about your current life circumstances with a balanced perspective, acknowledging your challenges and also your blessings. Look for one thing you can be grateful for. Write it down. Thank God for it. Continue to thank Him for every good thing until joy springs forth in your soul.

TOPIC

Maintaining Peace by Giving Your Worries to God

SCRIPTURES

1. **1 Peter 5:6,7** — Therefore humble yourselves under the mighty hand of God, that He may exalt you in due time, casting all your care upon Him, for He cares for you.

2. **Matthew 11:28-30** — "Come to Me, all you who labor and are heavy laden, and I will give you rest. Take My yoke upon you and learn from Me, for I am gentle and lowly in heart, and you will find rest for your souls. For My yoke is easy and My burden is light."

3. **Matthew 6:25-30** — "Therefore I say to you, do not worry about your life, what you will eat or what you will drink; nor about your body, what you will put on. Is not life more than food and the body more than clothing? Look at the birds of the air, for they neither sow nor reap nor gather into barns; yet your heavenly Father feeds them. Are you not of more value than they? Which of you by worrying can add one cubit to his stature? So why do you worry about clothing? Consider the lilies of the field, how they grow: they neither toil nor spin; and yet I say to you that even Solomon in all his glory was not arrayed like one of these. Now if God so clothes the grass of the field, which today is, and tomorrow is thrown into the oven, will He not much more clothe you, O you of little faith?"

SYNOPSIS

How often do we let worries and problems linger in our minds to the point that we lose our peace? Because it's so easy for us to do, Jesus spent a good portion of Matthew 6 letting us know that we are loved and cared for by our Heavenly Father — far more so than the birds of the air or the flowers of the field that are here today and gone tomorrow.

The emphasis of this lesson:

One of the biggest threats to our peace is holding on to worry. Because God wants us to stay peaceful in hard times, He gives us the privilege of casting all our cares on Him, so that He can care for us.

Hold On To Peace By Casting Your Cares

Another important part of maintaining peace is choosing to cast our cares on the Lord. Because He loves us so much and has promised to take care of us, we can trust Him to watch out for us. Jesus said in Matthew 11:28-30:

> Come to Me, all you who labor and are heavy laden, and I will give you rest. Take My yoke upon you and learn from Me, for I am gentle and lowly in heart, and you will find rest for your souls. For My yoke is easy and My burden is light.

Jesus doesn't want us carrying a heavy load that keeps us overwhelmed with weight and exhaustion. He wants us to come to Him and give Him that load so He can take care of us. God gives us two pieces of instruction through the apostle Peter that go perfectly together. In First Peter 5:6 and 7, it says:

> Therefore humble yourselves under the mighty hand of God, that He may exalt you in due time, casting all your care upon Him, for He cares for you.

Why would we need to humble ourselves? Because if we believe that we can trust in ourselves for everything we need, then we're in a state of pride. When we're in pride, we have built a wall against Him in our heart that keeps Him from being able to work in our lives. The Bible says that God resists the proud, but gives grace to the humble (*see* James 4:6).

We must know that we are not the one with the answer, but *Jesus is*; and it's important to know that *before* we can cast our care. He is the One who gave His blood to purchase our freedom, peace, and provision. He is the One who sent the Holy Spirit. He is the One who lives on the inside of us and who is our Helper. We might have the questions, but He always has the answers.

Many years ago, Denise knew a family of believers who had an eleven-year-old girl, and the mother greatly loved God and her children. One day this little girl suddenly had no strength and was in a lot of pain, so she was taken to the hospital and it was discovered that she had a horrible case of spinal meningitis. At the hospital were several other children about the same age that had been attacked with that very same disease. They were all suffering, and some of them even died.

Do you know what that young girl's mother did? She humbled herself before the Lord, and said, "God, I don't know what to do; but You are my answer." God showed her the answer in that moment — she had to fight the fear that was trying to mess with her thinking. When she came against fear, faith came, and she said, "My daughter is going to live and not die. She will give praise to God and have a good report and a testimony!"

Because fear was now gone, faith was there. They laid hands on that little girl and prayed, and the next day she was released to go home from the hospital. She needed an answer, but for her to receive it, her mother had to humble herself and choose to trust God so she could hear His direction.

What Do I Do When I'm Overwhelmed?

What do you do when you're facing an impossible situation?

When the doctor says, "I don't know that I can do any more for you. I don't know if I can do any more for your child."

When the counselor says, "I hope I can help you, but I'm not sure I can."

When the bank statement says you don't have any money in that account.

When creditors are calling to collect bills that are past due?

If we hold on to pride in our heart, believing we are self-sufficient on our own, it's going to be much harder for us to cast our care on the Lord. But if we come to God with a humble heart like that young mother did, we can receive the answer from Him. Let's take another look at Jesus' words in Matthew 11:28-30:

> **"Come to Me, all you who labor and are heavy laden, and I will give you rest. Take My yoke upon you and learn from Me, for I am gentle and lowly in heart, and you will find rest for your souls. For My yoke is easy and My burden is light."**

The Lord doesn't want us to carry a heavy burden around; He wants us to come to Him with a humble attitude and recognize that He is the one with the answer. When we rely on His magnificent arms that are reaching out to us, encouraging us as we wait on Him to work, we will be lifted up above that problem. We will receive an answer.

Don't Let Pride Hold You Back

Many times, Denise has asked people, "Can I pray for you?" And they would say, "Oh no, it's not so bad," even though they were facing an impossible situation. So often, because of pride and the deception of our own heart, we believe that we're self-sufficient and we say, "Oh no, I don't need your prayer — I don't need help."

But when we humble ourselves and admit, "God, I can't do this," then we put ourselves in a position to receive help from the Lord and others. We can cast our care on the Lord, because He cares for us. One of the best examples of this is in Matthew 6:25 and 26, where Jesus said:

> **Therefore I say to you, do not worry about your life, what you will eat or what you will drink; nor about your body, what you will put on. Is not life more than food and the body more than clothing? Look at the birds of the air, for they neither sow nor reap nor gather into barns; yet your heavenly Father feeds them. Are you not of more value than they?**

You might be thinking, *That sounds silly — why would I look at the birds?* Because Jesus gave it as an example to show us why we don't need to worry. You might say, "Well, everyone worries, worry is not so bad." Think again.

Denise knew of one woman who was constantly worrying about her finances, and she admitted that it opened the door for cancer to come into her life. Another lady she knows well, worried so much about her son that she had a heart attack. An obsessive, constant state of worry opens the door to the enemy, but Jesus paid the perfect, powerful, eternal price of His blood to free us from ALL of the enemy's traps. Thank You Jesus!

He instructs us with His counsel to look at the birds. In some commentaries, it says *look at, consider, study, pay attention to,* or *take knowledge of* the birds. Why are birds so special? Well, the Bible says that they neither sow nor reap; they don't even gather into barns, yet our Heavenly Father feeds them.

Look at the birds — they do not labor, they're not worried. Jesus is telling us to be encouraged by considering the birds. It might sound so simple, but Jesus — who was both 100 percent God and 100 percent man —had the answers for the people He was teaching, and that includes us today.

Look at the Birds

You know how birds will hold on to a branch or a wire, the side of a building, or a rooftop? How do they hold on to that all night long? How do you suppose they sleep while holding still? If birds were anxious, they might be gripping ahold of that tree branch or telephone line so hard they could fall over or even wake themselves up because they're so worried. But they're not anxious — *no birds are ever anxious!*

Have you ever woken up in the middle of the night because you're so consumed with worry about something? Those thoughts linger in your mind and keep you awake; but they don't have to. Like the birds, you can sleep in peace at night, knowing your Heavenly Father will take care of you. We can find so much confidence and comfort in that promise! Jesus also said in Matthew 6:28-30:

> **"...Consider the lilies of the field, how they grow: they neither toil nor spin; and yet I say to you that even Solomon in all his glory was not arrayed like one of these. Now if God so clothes the grass of the field, which today is, and tomorrow is thrown into the oven, will He not much more clothe you, O you of little faith?"**

Jesus said to look at the lilies of the field. They don't work or produce — and even though they only exist for a short while — God has clothed them in petals more beautiful than the clothes of any king in a palace. He also asked this question in verse 27:

> **Which of you by worrying can add one cubit to his stature?**

How empty and fruitless is it for someone to worry themselves into a frenzy, thinking that by doing so, they can make themselves grow taller? What would you say to a person like that? *"Give it up! Just because you are worrying about it will not make you any taller!"* Here, Jesus is saying that when we worry, it has no more productivity than someone constantly worrying about their height and wishing they were taller.

The Holy Spirit is inviting us to a place He wants us to be in, where we have peace during difficult times, and aren't weighed down or taken in by worry and care. If we feel weary and heavy-laden with worry, responsibility and weight, when we come to Jesus, recognizing He alone is our answer, we will find rest in His loving presence. A good prayer to pray when we're overwhelmed is:

Father, You know I've tried to figure this out myself, and I'm not getting any answers. Lord, I recognize that YOU are God and You have the answer. It was Your blood that saved me, heals me, and gives me protection and peace of mind. I'm trusting in You right now, and the sacrifice that You made for me. In Jesus' name, Amen.

We need to go outside and do what Jesus said: look at the birds. This is how we can maintain peace in difficult times...by casting our care on the Lord.

Denise's prayer for you:

Father, I thank You for my friends and for Your Holy Spirit living on the inside of them. Thank You for giving them grace and wisdom when they humble themselves before You. Help us to genuinely cast our care on You, because You care for us, and we will receive Your answer. Father, we love and appreciate You and thank You so much for Your help in our lives. In the powerful name of Jesus we pray, Amen.

STUDY QUESTIONS

**Be diligent to present yourself approved to God, a worker who does not need to be ashamed, rightly dividing the word of truth.
— 2 Timothy 2:15**

1. The best and only way to receive God's help and answers is through an attitude of humility. Which military leader in the Old Testament understood this firsthand (*see* 2 Kings 5:1-19)? What stands out to you most about his story?

2. In the same way, God sent the prophet Elijah to someone who was worried about how she and her son would survive a drought. Who was she, and what was the answer God gave to her need that didn't seem to make sense (*see* 1 Kings 17:7-16)? What does this tell you about God's character and His ability to work in the middle of difficult circumstances?

PRACTICAL APPLICATION

But be doers of the word,
and not hearers only, deceiving yourselves.
—James 1:22

1. How do you normally handle a problem that feels too big for you to solve? Does that care sit heavily on your mind for a while? Do you feel like it's your job to figure it out?

2. Which care(s) in your life tends to be the most difficult to cast on to the Lord? Take a minute to write out the first few that come to mind. Ask Him to help you release those weights to Him, one at a time. As you continue to do so, it will become easier and more natural to give those to Him, and your heart will become lighter and freer.

LESSON 10

TOPIC

Maintaining Peace by Recognizing the Real Enemy

SCRIPTURES

1. **Ephesians 6:12** — For we do not wrestle against flesh and blood, but against principalities, against powers, against the rulers of the darkness of this age, against spiritual hosts of wickedness in the heavenly places.

2. **Ephesians 1:20-22** — ...Christ when He raised Him from the dead and seated Him at His right hand in the heavenly places, far above all principality and power and might and dominion, and every name that is named, not only in this age but also in that which is to come. And He put all things under His feet, and gave Him to be head over all things to the church.

3. **Ephesians 2:6** — ...and made us sit together in the heavenly places in Christ Jesus....

4. **Daniel 6:21,22** — Then Daniel said to the king, "O king, live forever! My God sent His angel and shut the lions' mouths, so that they

have not hurt me, because I was found innocent before Him; and also, O king, I have done no wrong before you."

5. **John 14:27** — Peace I leave with you, My peace I give to you; not as the world gives do I give to you. Let not your heart be troubled, neither let it be afraid.

6. **Proverbs 15:1** — A soft answer turns away wrath....

SYNOPSIS

As believers, our real enemy is Satan, and he loves to deceive us into thinking that people are our problem. When they hurt, annoy, betray, or attack us, stand in our way, or refuse to give us what we hope for, it can be easy to look at the humans in front of us and lose our peace thinking that *they* are the ones we are fighting with — but in reality, our enemy is much more sinister and much less visible than we realize.

The emphasis of this lesson:

It is so important to remember that the people around us are not our enemy — that mindset can keep us in a state of feeling overwhelmed. Instead, when we recognize that our true enemy is Satan, we can remain calm with difficult people and trust God to fight for us.

Seeing Our Real Enemy

In the past several lessons, we have learned about controlling our emotions, the importance of forgiveness, avoiding complaining and focusing on the good, casting our care on the Lord, and how all of these behaviors help us hold on to peace in difficult times. This lesson is all about knowing who your real enemy *is* and knowing who it *isn't*. We need to know who we are truly fighting against.

When we're encountering problem after problem, it can be so easy to think that our battle is with the person or circumstance right in front of us. We might be having an issue at our workplace, with a family member, our spouse, a complicated situation, or an illness; in any case, it's incredibly important that we know how to respond effectively.

The Bible says we are not fighting against flesh and blood, but we're fighting against something and someone that we cannot see. We're fighting against principalities, powers, and rulers over the darkness of this world. We don't want to make assumptions based on what we feel or see to determine what we should do — that would be like making decisions while looking through foggy lenses. But when we look through the clear lenses of the Word of God, we're going to find encouragement, strength, wisdom, and help to maintain peace in these difficult times.

We know the apostle Paul wrote the following in Ephesians 6:12, during a very difficult situation:

> **For we do not wrestle against flesh and blood, but against principalities, against powers, against the rulers of the darkness of this age, against spiritual hosts of wickedness in the heavenly places.**

He essentially said, "I'm not fighting against flesh and blood. I'm not fighting against the government, those who lied about me, deceived or betrayed me. I'm not fighting against the leaders that have me in this prison. My real fight is against principalities and powers — with evil spirits you don't see."

It's very important that we understand this principle, and that we learn the Bible and know how to use it, because it's one of our greatest weapons against the enemy. Knowing that the Scripture tells us who we are fighting — and that we have victory through Christ — gives us confidence to walk in His peace and stand strong, even in tough times.

Seated in Heavenly Places

So, how does knowing who our real enemy is make a difference in helping us hold on to our peace? Because that enemy is already defeated. Let's take a look at Ephesians 1:20-22. It says:

> **…Christ when He raised Him from the dead and seated Him at His right hand in the heavenly places, far above all principality and power and might and dominion, and every name that is named, not only in this age but also in that which is to come. And He put all things under His feet, and gave Him to be head over all things to the church.**

Now consider Ephesians 2:6, which says that Jesus has raised us up with Himself "…and made us sit together [with Him] in the heavenly places in Christ Jesus."

Because Jesus gave us right standing with the Father through His blood, we are seated with Him in that position in heavenly places. We are not only seated *with Him*, but we are *in Him*. Greater is He that is in us than he that is in the world (*see* 1 John 4:4). And because of where you are seated in Christ, you have authority over any problem, situation, or seemingly indescribable odds that are waging war against you. Romans 8:11 declares that inside of you is the resurrection power of Christ. So, the One inside you is Greater than all that is coming against you. Know that you are *in Christ, seated with Him*, so you are above all the strategies of Satan.

Friend, we can take such a confident stand in Christ, because He lives in us. We don't need to be anxious or fearful because we are seated with Him in heavenly places *far above* all principalities and powers. The truth is, whatever comes against us has already been conquered by Jesus. So, when we recognize that the Greater One is in us, and He's greater than the storm raging around us, we can have peace in that storm, no matter how terrifying it is.

This great, conquering peace we have access to is not passive in any way; but when we maintain our peace, it's very aggressive against our enemy and conquers all our foes. In Scripture, we have examples of those who faced incredibly difficult situations and overwhelming odds, but they stood in the peace and power of God in those difficult times and they were able to overcome.

Hold Your Peace, Win the Battle

In a previous lesson, we read about David in First Samuel 17. The Bible doesn't say that David saw Goliath and started to back down exclaiming, "Oh no — I didn't know it was going to be that bad!" Even when Goliath tried to intimidate David with every single word, David held on to the peace of God inside him, that conquering peace, because David knew his enemy was already defeated.

There is a story about three Hebrews in the book of Daniel. There was a law that everyone had to bow down and worship a golden image of King Nebuchadnezzar, or they would be thrown into a fiery furnace. Well, it was discovered that Shadrach, Meshach and Abed-Nego were not worshiping the golden image, so they called them into the presence of the king. He basically said to them, "All you need to do is bow before my image and you won't be cast into the furnace," but they continued to do the right thing and refused to worship him. They were bold in their declaration, saying, "Even if God doesn't save us from the flames, we are not going to bow before your image." Then God showed up in power and might and rescued them in an unforgettable way (*see* Daniel 3:1-30).

Do you see the confidence and peace they had in their God, knowing He was more powerful than their enemy? That same God — who is in you — is so much greater than anything the enemy could ever throw at you. That is the same confidence and peace we see in David as he stood against the giant and conquered him, and all of Israel knew that God was for them.

There is also a great story of deliverance that came to a man named Daniel. He had enemies that plotted to trap him by getting the king to sign a decree — it said if anyone prayed to someone other than the king, they were to be thrown into a den of lions. Daniel received news that the decree had been signed, yet he boldly threw open the windows of his house and continued to pray to his God three times a day as he had always done (*see* Daniel 6:1-23).

When his enemies revealed his disobedience to the king, the king was greatly distressed. But when he called Daniel in to stand before him, he said, "Daniel, I've signed this law which cannot be changed, and it says if you do not stop praying then I have to throw you into the lions' den." He reluctantly gave the order and sealed the den and it was done.

The Bible says the king refused to eat and didn't sleep all night. The next morning, the king was anxious to find out if Daniel survived. The first thing he did was to unseal the den and call out to Daniel, asking him if his God had been powerful enough to rescue him. This was his reply in Daniel 6:21 and 22:

> **Then Daniel said to the king, "O king, live forever! My God sent His angel and shut the lions' mouths, so that they have not hurt me, because I was found innocent before Him; and also, O king, I have done no wrong before you."**

Daniel had absolute confidence because he knew his enemy was already defeated. That is where you and I are — that is the exact position our God has put us in, through the death, burial, and resurrection of our Lord Jesus Christ. It is a position of authority and honor, seated with Him, knowing that our enemies are under our feet.

Unshakable Peace

This peace that we have received from Him — it's not a natural peace. It empowers us to fight back against the enemy, whom Jesus has already defeated. Instead of running in fear, we can stand up against the devil's attacks and refuse to run, because we have access to that firm foundation of peace. Jesus said in John 14:27:

> **Peace I leave with you, My peace I give to you; not as the world gives do I give to you. Let not your heart be troubled, neither let it be afraid.**

This is a verse that we can receive right now, from Jesus Himself. Do you see His compassion, care, love, and comfort in those words as He comes alongside us? Another amazing verse in Proverbs really demonstrates how powerful peace is against your enemy. In Proverbs 15:1, it says that a soft answer turns away wrath. It is a *soft* answer that turns away wrath — not an argumentative one. A word spoken in peace, stands precisely in calmness and serenity. And because peace is more powerful than anger, it resists wrath. Rather than being pulled into an unnecessary conflict, peace stands up and says, *"No, I'm not going to wrestle with you."* Instead, it answers from the deepest part of your spirit. Knowing your enemy is defeated is what allows you to grab and hold on to your peace even during difficult circumstances.

The Word of God is such a gift. Psalm 119:105 says it is a lamp to our feet and a light to our path. When darkness crosses our path, the Word shines on that darkness, reminding us of who our enemy is and that he was defeated at the Cross. That is what will give us power and strength to maintain peace in difficult times.

Remember Who You Are in Christ

It is so important, friend, that we know the Word of God — that we know who our enemy is, and who it isn't. A lot of people spend their time, energy, and money fighting against people, when their real fight is with principalities and powers — spirits of darkness that we don't see.

The apostle Paul truly understood this truth. He had a lot of enemies he could have been focused on, but he knew they were not really his enemy. Paul knew his enemy was not the emperor who put him in prison, nor the one who lied about him or betrayed him — his fight, too, was with the principalities and powers that his real enemy, the devil, had sent against him. But the confidence he had in knowing Christ had put those enemies under his feet, enabled him to keep going through every kind of battle.

The Bible says you are seated in heavenly places with Christ *far above* your enemies. You have the authority to come against anything that's coming against you — just like David, Shadrach, Meshach, Abed-Nego, Daniel, the apostle Paul, and Jesus — you can stand and say, "No, I'm not fighting flesh and blood. I'm fighting principalities and powers, and because of what Jesus has done for me and because of who I am in Him, *I have authority* and I'm taking that authority right now (*see* Luke 10:19). In Jesus' name, you were defeated at the cross and I refuse to let you have an inch of ground in my life. No weapon formed against me will prosper (*see* Isaiah 54:17)!"

Denise's prayer for you:

> Father, I thank you so much for the Word of God and how the Holy Spirit emboldens us to stand up against our enemy as we refuse to be taken down by his lies or strategies. Thank You that we have the Greater One on the inside of us because you've placed us in Christ. We are seated with You in heavenly places far above our enemies. Lord, I thank You for the power of the Holy Spirit that's speaking to my friends right now, empowering and strengthening them to stand up and take their place. And for the peace You give us will sustain us in difficult times because we know who we are really fighting against. I thank You also for Your presence that's with us every single moment, never leaving nor forsaking us. I pray these things in Jesus' name, amen.

STUDY QUESTIONS

Be diligent to present yourself approved to God, a worker who does not need to be ashamed, rightly dividing the word of truth.
— 2 Timothy 2:15

1. Shadrach, Meshach and Abed-Nego had a genuine awareness of who their enemy was *and* who it wasn't. What stands out to you the most about their boldness, their story, or their confrontation of the king (*see* Daniel 3:8-30)?

2. When we have the correct awareness that our enemy is not any physical person, where should we focus our time and energy instead? How can we prepare well to fight our actual enemy (*see* Ephesians 6:10-18)?

PRACTICAL APPLICATION

But be doers of the word,
and not hearers only, deceiving yourselves.
—James 1:22

1. Who do you typically think of as your enemy? A friend who abandoned you? A parent who says deeply hurtful things? A boss who won't let you advance?
2. Now, slow down and reflect on the message that you feel you've received from that person. It might be something like, "You're not capable" or, "You're unattractive" or, "You're unworthy." Who do you think is the author of that lie?
3. Lastly, bring any of those persistent thoughts to God, asking Him to heal your heart and replace the lie with His truth. Know that you are deeply loved and valued by Him, and allow that truth to equip you to fight your real enemy.

LESSON 11

TOPIC

Maintaining Peace by Living One Day at a Time

SCRIPTURES

1. **Matthew 6:34** — Therefore do not worry about tomorrow, for tomorrow will worry about its own things. Sufficient for the day is its own trouble.
2. **Exodus 16:20,21** — Notwithstanding they did not heed Moses. But some of them left part of it until morning, and it bred worms and stank. And Moses was angry with them. So they gathered it every

morning, every man according to his need. And when the sun became hot, it melted.

3. **Matthew 6:11** — Give us this day our daily bread.

4. **Lamentations 3:22,23** — Through the Lord's mercies we are not consumed, Because His compassions fail not. They are new every morning; Great is Your faithfulness.

SYNOPSIS

For most of us, today's world is hectic and jampacked with activity. There always seems to be something to do and not enough time to do it. If we add the instability of society to this thinking, as well as the continuing moral meltdown that surrounds us, we have all the conditions needed to ignite anxiety, worry, and fear.

To maintain peace in such circumstances, we need to learn how to live one day at a time. Yesterday is gone, and tomorrow has not happened yet. All we really have is *today*, and that is what we are to focus on. If we let Him, God will show us how to tap into the power and peace of keeping our attention on the present day.

The emphasis of this lesson:

God longs for us to trust Him and abide in fellowship with Him daily. He will provide everything we need for each new day, but trying to guarantee provisions for tomorrow and beyond will result in a life of struggle. Learning to trust and rest in God for our daily needs helps us to maintain peace, even in difficult times.

Jesus Encouraged Living One Day at a Time

God's supernatural power is available to us to do anything He has called us to do — and the measure we need is given just one day at a time. Wisdom and strength for tomorrow's problems will be provided *tomorrow*, so today is what we need to give our attention to. Jesus said it this way in Matthew 6:34:

> **Therefore do not worry about tomorrow, for tomorrow will worry about its own things. Sufficient for the day is its own trouble.**

All the power you need for today is yours for the asking. But trying to resolve tomorrow's issues with today's energy is a waste of time. Jesus said not to worry about tomorrow but to concentrate on today. *The Message* version of the Bible renders that same Scripture in this way:

> **Give your entire attention to what God is doing right now, and don't get worked up about what may or may not happen tomorrow. God will help you deal with whatever hard things come up when the time comes.**

When we focus on what is in front of us, moment by moment, one day at a time, we are entering a life-giving mindset that is established by God. When tomorrow arrives, God will still be there and will help you deal with whatever comes your way. You have His Word on it!

Works Done Out of Worry Do Not Produce Anything Good

Have you read Exodus 16 when the Israelites were in the wilderness after being delivered from Egypt? It was at that time that God miraculously provided them with manna to eat. Manna, which literally means *what is it*, rained down from Heaven daily for six days a week. God instructed Moses to tell the people they were to gather what each of them needed for that day and no more — except for the sixth day when they were told to gather enough for the Sabbath, a day He told them to set aside for rest and no work (*see* Exodus 16:15-26).

Unfortunately, not everyone listened to God's instructions. Exodus 16:20 says, "Notwithstanding they did not heed Moses. But some of them left part of it until morning, and it bred worms and stank." God wanted the people to obey and trust Him for what they needed each day. But out in the wilderness, worry set in and caused a number of the Israelites to gather several days' worth of manna at one time. The excess they collected produced worms — more commonly known as maggots.

There is an important principle to learn here, and that is when we live life doing things our way instead of by His guidance, our extra efforts done in the flesh don't really produce what we intend. But if we will obey what God tells us and trust Him for the provision and answers we need daily, we will have everything we need, right when we need it.

Denise Struggled To Trust God for the Anointing To Sing

On the program, Denise shared how there was a time in her life when she struggled to live one day at a time — especially when it came to using her ministry gift in the area of singing. Many years ago, when people would ask her to sing at an event, she would accept the invitation. Although it may not take place for weeks or several months, she would immediately begin worrying about how it was going to turn out.

Of course, she needed to prepare for the event by practicing the songs — the problem was she would constantly wonder if she was preparing enough and what would be the outcome. She found it very difficult to trust God and live peacefully one day at a time.

Just as some of the Israelites struggled to trust God to provide the bread they needed for that day, Denise struggled to believe that God would provide the physical strength and vocal ability she would need on the day she was scheduled to sing. For some reason, she was afraid that when the time came, the anointing of God, which she had experienced so many times before, would just not show up this time.

What if this happens? she thought. *Or what if that happens?*

If you've ever gone down the "what if" road, you know it never ends. Scenario after scenario of negative outcomes begin to play on the screen in your mind, and the more you watch and meditate on them, the more troubled and weary you become. Does this sound familiar? Has it been difficult for you to trust God to come through on something you needed Him for?

Well, you don't have to stay in a pit of despair. Like Denise and countless others, you can choose to recognize the power of the Holy Spirit living inside you, surrender your situation to Him, and begin to rest in His faithfulness. He will empower you to tackle whatever comes that day as you lean on Him in trust.

God Gives Us *Daily* Bread

When Jesus taught His disciples how to pray, He included the principle of living one day at a time. In Matthew 6:9-11 He said, "In this manner, therefore, pray: Our Father in heaven, Hallowed be Your name. Your kingdom come. Your will be done on earth as it is in heaven." He then continued, "Give us this day our *daily* bread."

Notice Jesus doesn't ask the Father for our "monthly" bread or even our "weekly" bread. Just like the provision of manna for the Israelites in the wilderness was daily, the provision that comes from God in our lives is also *daily*. Again, our Heavenly Father is looking for ongoing fellowship with us in a relationship of trust. He wants us to trust and rest in Him, knowing that He will provide for all our needs as a good Father does.

It is also important to note that as we have talked about living one day at a time, that does not mean we ignore things that are coming and neglect to plan for them. The Bible says, "A prudent man foresees the difficulties ahead and prepares for them…" (*see* Proverbs 22:3 *TLB*). It is wise to be aware of things that are coming and to do whatever our part is to prepare. We are simply not to be weighed down with worry and anxiety over the future.

Receive encouragement once more from the words of Jesus, "So do not worry or be anxious about tomorrow, for tomorrow will have worries and anxieties of its own. Sufficient for each day is its own trouble" (*see* Matthew 6:34 *AMPC*).

God's Mercies Are New Every Day

This principle of living one day at a time is also found in the book of Lamentations. Here, the Holy Spirit moved on the prophet Jeremiah, prompting him to write these amazing words:

> **Through the Lord's mercies we are not consumed, because His compassions fail not. They are new every morning; Great is Your faithfulness.**
>
> **— Lamentations 3:22,23**

Every morning you wake up, God provides brand new mercies for that day. They are like beautifully wrapped gifts right at the foot of your bed. What are His mercies? They consist of *not* getting what you deserve.

- Have you ever run a red light and not gotten a ticket? *That was mercy.*

- Have you ever been around people who were very sick and not caught it? *That was mercy.*

- Have you ever been impatient or harsh with others, but God was not harsh and impatient with you? *That was mercy.*

These examples barely scratch the surface of the mercies the Lord gives us each day. He gives us grace, kindness, forgiveness, protection, and deliverance in so many areas that if we became aware of them all, we would be utterly astonished.

Realize that the mercies God gives you are unique to who you are or your situation and may not be the same as what He gives to others. Each day you can pray, "Thank You Father, for Your mercies that are new every morning. I take them by faith and am truly grateful for Your kindness towards me. Praise Your mighty Name!"

Jesus Lived One Day at a Time

Think about Jesus for a moment. If anyone could have worried about tomorrow, it would have been Him. He faced many difficult challenges throughout His life. After His baptism, He was led into the wilderness where He went without food for 40 days and was tempted by the devil (*see* Luke 4:1-13). As He began His ministry, He was ridiculed, hated, and condemned by religious leaders on a regular basis. Again and again, they tried to lay a trap for Him so they could bring legal charges against Him and stone Him to death.

Because Jesus knew the Old Testament prophecies, He knew what He would eventually have to face as the chosen Messiah sent by God:

- The rejection of the Jewish leaders (*see* Isaiah 53:3, Luke 9:22)
- Judas' ultimate betrayal (*see* Psalm 41:9, John 18:2)
- Peter's denial (*see* Zechariah 13:7, Matthew 26:69-75)
- And the desertion of all His disciples in His greatest hour of need (*see* Psalm 31:11, Mark 14:27)

Jesus also knew the punishment He would receive from the Romans and the pieces of metal, glass, and bone fragments that would tear into His flesh, so that by those stripes we could be healed (*see* Isaiah 53:5, 1 Peter 2:24). He knew about the Cross and the large spikes that would be driven through His hands and feet — that He would hang between two criminals, pushing Himself up on those spikes as He gasped for every breath. He knew that after He died, He would be in the grave for three days during which time He would descend into hell itself. (*see* Psalm 16:10, Revelation 1:18)

What do you suppose could have happened if Jesus lived His life worrying about tomorrow? If He had not taken hold of the mercies, wisdom, and strength that God offered Him with each new day, He would not have been effective in what was set before Him.

Live in the Power of Today!

Jesus lived one day at a time and He is our example. It is this wisdom He wants us to walk in so we can take hold of the peace and power that's available to us for each new day.

Friend, there is great strength in waking up every morning and giving your entire attention to what is before you. He promises to give you the grace — His supernatural power — to live one day at a time, and it is this mindset that enables you to maintain peace, even in difficult times.

Do you need God's wisdom to deal with family, health, or financial issues? Are there situations on your job, with your boss, or a coworker that you need God's grace to understand and navigate? Whatever you need today is available *today* — just ask Him for it and receive it by faith.

There may be a part of you that really wants to worry about tomorrow, but the Spirit of God wants you to submit to His Word and say, "I receive every bit of mercy, energy, power, and grace the Holy Spirit is giving me today." That is the kind of decision Jesus made and the resolve He had every single day. If you will apply it too, it will help you walk in peace every day of your life.

Denise's prayer for you:

> Father, I pray with my friends right now, that we truly submit ourselves to Your amazing truth from our hearts, and that we take hold of these mercies that are there for us every single day. Lord, we look to You as our example. Just as You submitted Yourself to the Father, trusting Him for each new day, we pray that You will help us make that same decision — to live just one day at a time. I pray this in Jesus' name. Amen.

STUDY QUESTIONS

**Be diligent to present yourself approved to God, a worker
who does not need to be ashamed, rightly dividing the word of truth.
— 2 Timothy 2:15**

1. One good guideline to follow in receiving and living in the peace of God is found in Philippians 4:6-8. Take some time to meditate on this wisdom from Heaven and in your own words, write out what the Holy Spirit is speaking to you personally from this passage.

2. It is the desire of your Heavenly Father for you to absolutely know that He loves you and will take care of you every day. Consider the following scriptures and seriously think about what the Holy Spirit is showing you through them. How do these verses help you trust God knowing that He loves you?

    - Matthew 6:25-34

    - Romans 8:31-39

    - 2 Corinthians 9:8-11

    - Philippians 4:19

    - Ephesians 3:16-21

    - 1 Peter 5:7

PRACTICAL APPLICATION

**But be doers of the word,
and not hearers only, deceiving yourselves.
— James 1:22**

1. Have you ever tried to live more than one day at a time? Have you been anxious, worried, or fearful about something that "might" happen in the days ahead? If so, how did it affect you?

2. Are you worried or fearful about something right now? Why not take it to God and pray about it. Simply surrender that concern to your Heavenly Father, asking Him to show you what to do and then ask for His grace to trust Him and rest in His peace.

3. Imagine what your life might be like if you began to get up every day without worry or fear. How much more energy and peace would you experience in your mind and heart? How would your health be

affected in a positive way? Pray and ask the Lord to help you begin living life *one day at a time* — casting your care onto Him and receiving His grace and mercy to do what He's called you to do.

LESSON 12

TOPIC

Maintaining Peace by Guarding Your Thoughts

SCRIPTURES

1. **Proverbs 23:7** — For as he thinks in his heart, so is he....

2. **John 16:33** — These things I have spoken to you, that in Me you may have peace. In the world you will have tribulation; but be of good cheer, I have overcome the world.

3. **2 Corinthians 10:4,5** — For the weapons of our warfare are not carnal but mighty in God for pulling down strongholds, casting down arguments and every high thing that exalts itself against the knowledge of God, bringing every thought into captivity to the obedience of Christ.

4. **Psalm 2:1-4** — Why do the nations rage, and the people plot a vain thing? The kings of the earth set themselves, and the rulers take counsel together, against the Lord and against His Anointed, saying, "Let us break their bonds in pieces and cast away their cords from us." He who sits in the heavens shall laugh; the Lord shall hold them in derision.

5. **Daniel 5:23** — ...And you have praised the gods of silver and gold, bronze and iron, wood and stone, which do not see or hear or know; and the God who holds your breath in His hand and owns all your ways, you have not glorified.

6. **1 Peter 2:24** — Who Himself bore our sins in His own body on the tree, that we, having died to sins, might live for righteousness — by whose stripes you were healed.

7. **Philippians 4:8** — Finally, brethren, whatever things are true, whatever things are noble, whatever things are just, whatever things are

pure, whatever things are lovely, whatever things are of good report, if there is any virtue and if there is anything praiseworthy — meditate on these things.

SYNOPSIS

Without exception, it is God's will that you walk in peace throughout your life, even in difficult circumstances. The Bible says that Jesus is the *Prince of Peace*, and it is one of the primary manifestations of His Spirit inside you (*see* Galatians 5:22). Clearly, God wants you to live in His peace.

One of the greatest ways to maintain peace in difficult times is by *managing your thoughts*. Proverbs 23:7 says, "For as he [any person] thinks in his heart, so is he…." This brings us to the all-important question: "What are you thinking about on a regular basis?" God wants you to learn to recognize and reject wrong thoughts and choose to think right ones. How this is done is what we will focus on in this lesson.

The emphasis of this lesson:

Wrong thinking is a major cause for a lack of peace. The enemy seeks to build strongholds of ungodly thoughts in our minds, but we can destroy them by using the powerful spiritual weapons God has given us.

What's on Your Mind?

An important habit to practice on a daily basis is to *think about what you are thinking about*. In other words, what kinds of thoughts are regularly revolving around in your mind? Jesus said, "…Out of the abundance of the heart the mouth speaks" (*see* Matthew 12:34). This reveals that the things you are thinking about will also be what you are talking about, because the mouth is the release valve of what is in the heart.

Let's say you really want to lose weight, but all of your efforts are not producing results. It would be good for you to stop and ask, "Lord, what am I thinking, believing, and saying about my weight?" Remember the Scripture that says, as a person thinks in his heart, so is he. Are you thinking and saying things like, "I'll never lose weight. I'll always be this size. Everyone in my family is overweight, so why should I think I'm going to be any different"?

If you are, your thoughts and words are working against your God-given desire to be healthy. But with the help of the Holy Spirit, you can begin to think and speak differently and put an end to these self-sabotaging ways.

The same is true about every other area of your life. If you want to see improvements in an area but seem to be stuck and getting nowhere, it is important to stop and ask yourself what you are thinking, believing, and saying about those situations. Once the Holy Spirit shows you, ask Him to help you retrain your brain to think and speak in line with what God's Word says about them.

Overcoming the World Begins With Winning the Battle Within

Some of the last words Jesus spoke to His disciples before going to the Cross are found in John's gospel. Let's look at John 16:33, where Jesus said, "These things I have spoken to you, that in Me you may have peace. In the world you will have tribulation; but be of good cheer, I have overcome the world."

One of the ways we "overcome the world" is by gaining control over our thoughts. This means agreeing with the thoughts that line up with God's Word and discarding the thoughts that don't. The Bible says that God has given us spiritual weapons, and "...the weapons of our warfare are not carnal but mighty in God for pulling down strongholds" (*see* 2 Corinthians 10:4).

In the original Greek language, the word "strongholds" in this verse describes *a fortified castle* with thick, impenetrable walls. In the context of this Scripture, it depicts *a castle of thoughts* that is built up in the mind over a period of time. To defeat wrong thinking and win the battle in our minds, we must identify ungodly strongholds and demolish them with the mighty spiritual weapons God has given us.

How Are Strongholds Built?

Now that we know what a stronghold is, let's look at how it gets built. To help us understand this process, let's go back to our example of a person who is trying to lose weight but seems to be stuck. Just as a wall is built one brick at a time, so a mental stronghold is built one thought at a time. Look again at this internal conversation:

- Thought #1: *I'll never lose weight.*

- Thought #2: *I'll always be this size.*

- Thought #3: *Everyone in my family is overweight, so why should I think I'm going to be any different?*

Each thought is like a "brick" handed to this person, and if that person *accepts* the thought, another brick is added to their fortress wall. The enemy offers us brick after brick — *thought after thought* — with the goal of building a fortress of wrong thinking in our minds through which he can operate and influence our life.

To fortify the stronghold, he will also inject fearful and condemning thoughts into our minds. In the case of the person wanting to lose weight, those thoughts may be:

- *Oh, no! I keep gaining weight. I'll never be the size I want to be!*

- *Who is ever going to want to marry me looking the way I look?*

- *You have absolutely no self-control. You'll never be able to say no to the wrong foods.*

- *You are an embarrassment to God and your family. You ought to be ashamed of yourself.*

Every time we accept these thoughts of judgment, criticism, and condemnation, we add bricks to the stronghold, making it more fixed than before. Keep in mind, there are all kinds of strongholds. It is the plan of the enemy to create solid fortresses of ungodly thinking in different areas of our lives, especially in our understanding of God.

The Enemy Comes Against Us With Very Clever Arguments

Looking once more at Second Corinthians 10:4, it says, "For the weapons of our warfare are not carnal but mighty in God for pulling down strongholds." The weapons He has given us are spiritual and they are mighty! We learned in a previous lesson that our fight is not with those in the physical realm that we *can* see, it's really with evil spirits in the spirit realm that we *don't* see. Because of this, the weapons we have been given are mighty for fighting in that realm.

In Second Corinthians 10:5, the Bible continues on this subject by identifying the types of bricks that make up a stronghold — they are "…arguments and every high thing that exalts itself against the knowledge of God…."

The word "arguments" is translated in some versions as *imaginations*, and it describes *intellectual reasoning*, *arguments*, or *a judgment that makes sense to the mind*.

This lets us know that the thoughts the enemy brings against our mind are extremely clever and appear to be filled with wisdom. Nevertheless, these arguments are deceptions, and they are often accompanied by anything that has lifted itself up against the knowledge of God.

God Is Greater Than Any Power in the World or Stronghold in Your Mind

Regardless of what the enemy or an ungodly person tries to bring against you, they are no match for your Heavenly Father! Psalm 2 provides a unique perspective on what God thinks of the plots and plans of the enemy. It says:

> **Why do the nations rage, and the people plot a vain thing?**
>
> **The kings of the earth set themselves, and the rulers take counsel together, against the Lord and against His Anointed, saying, "Let us break their bonds in pieces and cast away their cords from us."**
>
> **He who sits in the heavens shall laugh; the Lord shall hold them in derision.**
>
> **— Psalm 2:1-4**

This passage lets us know that God is in no way intimidated by the ungodly establishment of this world. As they strategize their evil schemes, motivated by the enemy, He sits in Heaven and laughs because He knows their day of judgment is on its way, and they will not escape punishment.

A great example of this is found in the story of Belshazzar. He was a powerful king who reigned in Babylon during the time of Daniel. God's people had been taken into captivity years earlier, and Belshazzar kept the holy vessels that had been used in service to God in the Jewish Temple. One night when he and his guests were having a lavish party, he decided to use them to drink from.

The Bible says while Belshazzar and his companions were carelessly drinking wine out of those vessels, the hand of God appeared in the king's palace and wrote out an inscription on the palace wall. Paralyzed by fear,

Belshazzar called in all his astrologers, soothsayers, and magicians, but they couldn't decipher the writing.

Upon the queen's recommendation, Daniel was brought in to interpret the mysterious message. Daniel spoke respectfully to the king and said, "…You have praised the gods of silver and gold, bronze and iron, wood and stone, which do not see or hear or know; and the God who holds your breath in His hand and owns all your ways, you have not glorified" (*see* Daniel 5:23). Daniel gave the complete interpretation of the writing which declared that because of the king's pride and his worship of false gods, he was under God's judgment. That night Belshazzar was killed, and his kingdom taken over by the Medes and Persians. (You can read the whole story in Daniel chapter 5.)

Friend, God is above all, and He will not be mocked (*see* Galatians 6:7). He is not intimidated by His enemies, and He laughs at their efforts against Him. He wants you to have the same mindset regarding the devil's attacks because the very God who is not intimidated *lives in you*, and gives you the weapons you need to tear down these strongholds.

How Do We Pull Down Strongholds?

If you are dealing with a fortress in your mind, there is a way out! Although the world in which we live is saturated by evil and wickedness is on the rise, the Greater One lives in you (*see* 1 John 4:4)! There may be ungodly thoughts coming against your mind, but God has given you powerful tools to overcome them. They involve His *Word* and His *Spirit*, as well as *the Name* and *Blood of Jesus*. All these weapons are exceedingly powerful in Him! As you renew your mind to the Word of God daily (*see* Romans 12:2), He wants you to speak that Word against the enemy and over your life (*see* Jeremiah 23:28-29). You don't have to receive every impression that tries to invade your mind, you have been given authority over every thought that does not line up with the Word of God and through Him, you have the ability to resist it and throw it away before the seed of that thought begins to take root in your soul (*see* James 4:7).

Let's say you have prayed and asked the Holy Spirit to identify a stronghold in your life, and He has shown you what it is. You can take the situation to God and say, "Father, I ask you to forgive me for allowing the enemy to build a stronghold of _____ in my life. In the name of Jesus, I renounce every lie that built those walls and command the stronghold of

_____ to begin to break down and be destroyed. Father, I thank You for the truths You are showing me in Your Word, because it says that I shall know the truth, and the truth shall set me free. I am asking You to help me to recognize and reject any further lies from the enemy. In Jesus' name I pray, amen."

Now, when those thoughts come to your mind again, you are to stand *on* the Word of God and *against* the enemy. If he whispers things like…

You'll never get out of debt or be financially blessed.

You can say:

"God is able to bring every blessing to me in abundance so I always have more than enough! He supplies all my needs according to His riches in Heaven!" (*See* 2 Corinthians 9:8 *AMPC*, Philippians 4:19.)

If the devil tries to make you think…

You'll never lose weight. You're going to stay obese just like everybody else in your family. It's in your genes.

You can say:

"My body is the temple of the Holy Spirit, and He is my Helper and Guide! I receive His wisdom to resist temptation and choose the right foods for my body." (*See* 1 Corinthians 6:12,19-20; James 1:5; Psalm 25:12.)

No matter the lie that has been built in your mind, you don't have to sit back and accept it. Stand up and reject it! Dive deep into God's Word and discover what He has to say about the stronghold you are dealing with. Speak His Word out loud — against the enemy and over your life, in the name of Jesus — and the stronghold will break down and be destroyed!

Capture Every Ungodly Thought and Place It Under Arrest

How are we to deal with these thoughts that attempt to supersede and cancel out the Word of God in our lives? To complete our examination of Second Corinthians 10:5, it says we are to *cast down* those arguments, "…bringing every thought into captivity to the obedience of Christ." In the original Greek, this phrase "bringing into captivity" is the picture of a conqueror who takes his sword and presses the sharp point of it into the back of the person he's captured.

To help you understand what this looks like in a practical sense, imagine you are out around people who are sick, and a series of thoughts come against your mind, saying, *You better get ready to be sick. Everyone else is getting it, and you're no different than they are. Who are you to think you can escape catching this — it's highly contagious.*

These thoughts are *intellectual reasonings* and *arguments* trying to supersede what God's Word says. If you were to come under such an attack, you are to pull out your sword of the Spirit — the Word of God — and press it against the lies of the enemy. Yield to the power of the Holy Spirit inside you and say:

> "I take authority over those thoughts and speak the Word of God over my body. Jesus bore my sins in His own body on the tree, and by His stripes I have been healed (*see* 1 Peter 2:24). I take those thoughts captive, place them under arrest, and lock them up, in the name of Jesus."

That is what it looks like to bring wrong thoughts into captivity under the obedience of Christ. It is a picture of maintaining a defensive watch over your thoughts.

Choose Your Thoughts Carefully

In addition to taking a defensive stand against ungodly thoughts, we are also to take an *offensive* approach. This is laid out in Philippians 4:8, where the apostle Paul said:

> **Finally, brethren, whatever things are true, whatever things are noble, whatever things are just, whatever things are pure, whatever things are lovely, whatever things are of good report, if there is any virtue and if there is anything praiseworthy — meditate on these things.**

An effective way to stop thinking wrong thoughts is to simply *think another thought.* In this passage, we see that we can choose to think about:

- Things that are *true*
- Things that are *noble*

- Things that are *just*
- Things that are *pure*
- Things that are *lovely*
- Things that are *of good report*
- Things that are *virtuous*
- Things that are *worthy of praise*

Regardless of where you are in your walk with God, you can probably find at least one thing to think about in each of these eight categories. A good place to start would be to remember that Jesus is the Son of God who died for you and loves you so much. When you accepted Him, He gave you a new heart and sent the Holy Spirit to live in you. He is your Helper, Teacher and Guide and gives you strength for each new day. Each of these thoughts are true, of good report, and worthy of praise. When you choose these thoughts instead of negative ones, your heart is able to stay in peace. Choosing your own thoughts is an offensive weapon that is proven to be effective.

One other practical suggestion to consider is to avoid what is being broadcast on the Internet, news, or social media. The things that are being stated or publicized are not always true, and many times the goal is to get you caught up in the world's system and its way of thinking (*see* Ephesians 2:1,2). The Bible says that this world is passing away (*see* 1 John 2:15-17), but when you stay with the Word of God and His life-giving Spirit on the inside of you, you will avoid being swept away with the rest of the world and experience a greater level of peace, even in difficult times.

Denise's prayer for you:

> Father, I thank You that we have this opportunity to be together today, and for the power that is in Your Word. And Lord, we will not allow the enemy to have control over our thoughts, but by our own will we choose to take captive the thoughts that are trying to bring us down and steal our peace, and we choose to think about the things that are in Your Word. We thank You for the power of your Holy Spirit who is so present with us right now, and we give You all the praise. In Jesus' name, amen.

STUDY QUESTIONS

Be diligent to present yourself approved to God, a worker
who does not need to be ashamed, rightly dividing the word of truth.
— 2 Timothy 2:15

1. The weapons God has given you to fight against the enemy are spiritual, and they are powerful! These weapons include His *Word* and His *Spirit*, as well as *the Name* and *Blood of Jesus.* What do you know about these weapons? Consider the following scriptures and take some time to reflect on them. What other verses come to mind regarding the weapons God has given you?
    *   **The Word**: Hebrews 4:12; Jeremiah 23:29
    *   **The Spirit**: Romans 8:11; Galatians 5:16,22-25; Zechariah 4:6
    *   **The Name of Jesus**: John 14:13,14; Philippians 2:9-11
    *   **The Blood of Jesus**: Hebrews 9:11-14; 1 John 1:7; Revelation 12:11

2. What kind of authority have you been given through the finished work of Jesus? Check out these powerful promises for the answer and then ask the Holy Spirit to help you learn how to yield to Him and operate in His power.
    *   Luke 10:19
    *   Matthew 16:19; 18:18-20; 28:18-20
    *   Mark 16:15-18

PRACTICAL APPLICATION

But be doers of the word,
and not hearers only, deceiving yourselves.
— James 1:22

1. Is there an area of your life where you would like to see improvement? Based on Scripture, how would you like to see it advance?

2. Considering your answer to the question directly above, are you seeing positive change, or do you seem to be stuck with no results? Take a few moments to ask the Lord and reflect on what you are thinking, believing, and saying about that situation. Ask Him to help you renew your mind with His Word so that you begin to think and speak what it says about that area.

TOPIC

Maintaining Peace by Controlling Your Mouth

SCRIPTURES

1. **James 3:5** — Even so the tongue is a little member and boasts great things. See how great a forest a little fire kindles!

2. **James 1:19** — So then, my beloved brethren, let every man be swift to hear, slow to speak, slow to wrath.

3. **Proverbs 12:14,18** — A man will be satisfied with good by the fruit of his mouth, and the recompense of a man's hands will be rendered to him. There is one who speaks like the piercings of a sword, but the tongue of the wise promotes health.

4. **Proverbs 15:1** — A soft answer turns away wrath, but a harsh word stirs up anger.

5. **Proverbs 16:32** — He who is slow to anger is better than the mighty, and he who rules his spirit than he who takes a city.

6. **Proverbs 15:28** — The heart of the righteous studies how to answer, but the mouth of the wicked pours forth evil.

7. **Proverbs 16:23** — The heart of the wise teaches his mouth, and adds learning to his lips.

SYNOPSIS

In our last lesson, we talked about overcoming and avoiding strongholds in our lives by guarding our thoughts. In addition to recognizing and discarding wrong thoughts, we can also choose to think on things that are true, honest, just, and pure so we can maintain our peace in difficult times (*see* Philippians 4:8,9 *KJV*).

The Bible says in Proverbs 18:21 that death and life are in the power of the tongue. If you are not experiencing much peace in your life, the answer may be right under your nose. Are you speaking words of life and blessing or words of death and destruction? In these last of the last days,

God wants us to speak words of life over ourselves and every situation that comes our way.

The emphasis of this lesson:

To effectively control our mouths, we need to be quick to hear, slow to speak, and slow to become angry. Through the power of the Holy Spirit, we can study and reflect on how to answer and teach our lips to respond in a way which leads to greater peace in our lives.

Be Slow To Speak

The mouth is a small part of the body but despite its size, it packs great power. James 3:5 confirms this, saying, "Even so the tongue is a little member and boasts great things. See how great a forest a little fire kindles!" Has someone ever said something to you, and their few short words ignited something in you? That's how powerful the tongue is.

It is for this reason James also warns with these words: "So then, my beloved brethren, let every man be swift to hear, slow to speak, slow to wrath" (*see* James 1:19). God has given us two ears but only one mouth, which tells us that listening is twice as important as speaking.

If you have ever been around someone who is always talking and doesn't let anyone get a word in edgewise, you know how frustrating it can be. If you've been around individuals who talk incessantly and without thinking, it is both exasperating and heartbreaking. They just say anything that comes to their mind about anyone — including themselves. Their tongue is causing all kinds of destruction and they are totally oblivious to the effect of their words.

What Kind of Words Are You Eating?

Maybe you've heard it said, "You're going to eat those words." Well, there is a great deal of truth in that statement. Proverbs 12:14 confirms this to be true, which states:

> **A man will be satisfied with good by the fruit of his mouth, and the recompense of a man's hands will be rendered to him.**

This truth is repeated again in another chapter, which says, "A man's stomach shall be satisfied from the fruit of his mouth; from the produce of his lips he shall be filled" (*see* Proverbs 18:20).

These verses tell us that the words we speak are either going to be satisfying or dissatisfying to our souls. When we speak well of ourselves and others, our words are going to nourish our inward man, bringing peace and inspiration. But if we speak poorly — using our words to criticize, ridicule, and humiliate — our words are going to produce poison, bringing distress and destruction on ourselves and those around us. The truth is, we will either be content and fulfilled or dissatisfied and frustrated by the things that come out of our mouths.

Likewise, the Bible also tells us, "There is one who speaks like the piercings of a sword, but the tongue of the wise promotes health" (*see* Proverbs 12:18). Has anyone spoken sharply to you where it felt like "the piercings of a sword"? How about words of life that brought healing to your soul? Here again we see that our words are able to produce one or the other, depending on how we use them.

You have probably felt the effects of crushing, piercing words from others and know how painful words can be. Have you ever been the one speaking such words? Lord, help us be quick to listen, slow to speak, and aware of our own words *before* they come cascading out of our mouth.

There's Power in Answering Softly and Being Slow To Anger

Proverbs 15:1 tells us, "A soft answer turns away wrath, but a harsh word stirs up anger." This verse reveals just how powerful the tone of our words can be. Logically, no one would think or believe that a gentle, calm reply would be more effective than loud, harsh words when someone is angry — but it is. If someone is upset with you and yells abrasively, responding to them with kindness can diffuse that anger and rage and bring peace to the situation.

When you respond to harsh words with a quiet, pleasant tone of voice, wrath will be turned away. When you choose to say, "No, devil! I'm not going to let you use my tongue to speak words of criticism and anger. I'm going to give a gentle answer spoken in peace" — you will experience the presence of God on the inside of you, and bring His peace into the conversation.

Proverbs 16:32 encourages us further saying, "He who is slow to anger is better than the mighty, and he who rules his spirit than he who takes a city." Wow! Understand what God is saying here. We talked about this in a previous lesson, but it bears repeating — He is telling us that the one who is slow to anger is the one who rules his spirit. This is the fruit of *self-control*, and Scripture says one who operates in self-control is greater than a military warrior who conquers a city in battle.

There have been some amazing generals all throughout history who have achieved great victories. People like Alexander the Great, George Washington, and Napoleon Bonaparte, are revered as highly successful leaders who conquered lands. But in God's view, the one who rules his spirit — the one who operates in self-control — is deserving of equal, if not more, honor. That is how powerful being slow to anger and controlling our words is in God's eyes.

It is so important to be slow to speak and carefully choose our words. If instead we immediately give an angry reply, that will rapidly turn into a flowing river of poison that pours out of our mouths, and once that happens, the damage is done. Thankfully, we can learn to be slow to speak and quick to turn to the Holy Spirit for help. If you find yourself confronted by someone expelling cruel and angry words towards you, check your heart and ask the Lord to give you the right words for an answer that is enveloped in peace.

Study and Reflect Before You Answer

It's important that we learn how to be slow to speak and give a gentle answer in difficult situations. As with anything in life that we learn, it usually means that studying is involved. This brings us to Proverbs 15:28, which says, "The heart of the righteous studies how to answer, but the mouth of the wicked pours forth evil."

Maybe you're reading this lesson and you're in school or you've already gotten a degree. Either way, you understand that studying is the key to success! Whether you are learning about medicine or ministry, mechanical engineering or computer technology, you've realized how studying the subject was a major part of your achievement. The same is true for learning how to answer others in a godly way. Rather than just say whatever you feel like saying in the moment, this verse says that we are to study or reflect on how to answer.

On the program, Denise shared a real-life story that helps answer this question. For many years, she has taught classes on marriage for women, and there was one woman in those classes that was really struggling in her relationship with her husband. He was very harsh with her and for some reason, very angry.

There were times when he would get in his wife's face and tell her, "I hate you! And I don't want you in my life!" Needless to say, his words were crushing and devastating to her. But she was committed to God and faithfully coming to class, paying attention to the Scripture, and learning how to be a godly wife.

Well, as you might imagine, it wasn't long before she had another confrontation with her husband, and once again he got in her face and spoke words of hatred and disgust towards her. But this time she did something different. Immediately, she said, "Okay, I'm going to dismiss myself from this conversation," and she stepped away from her husband to consider how she should answer him.

She got quiet and prayed, "Lord, what do I say? What do I do?" She then calmed herself down, walked back into the conversation, looked at her husband and softly said, "Sweetheart, I love you and I'm praying for you."

Shocked by her response, he stood and looked at her in amazement. All of a sudden, he said, "I am so sorry." He wrapped his arms around her and hugged her.

In time, that marriage was saved because this woman made a decision to reflect on her answer before responding to her husband. Without question, the normal, human response to your spouse screaming words of hatred and rejection in your face is to retaliate and walk away. But that's not what this person did. Instead of letting her mouth say whatever she thought or felt like saying, she humbled herself before God and asked Him for help in what to say and do. Her life was satisfied because of the words of her mouth.

The Wise Teach Their Mouth How To Respond

Friend, you may not have the ability as this person did to walk away from a confrontation for a few minutes to pray, but if you will study the Word ahead of time and get it deep into your heart, you will have the answer from the Lord when you need it (*see* Psalm 119:11). This is a good routine to develop. Proverbs 16:23 tells us:

The heart of the wise teaches his mouth, and adds learning to his lips.

If someone is verbally assaulting you with criticism and insults, and you're tempted to respond in the same manner, hold on to your peace, surrender yourself to God, and teach your mouth what to say.

You can start just by looking in the mirror and simply smiling at yourself. When you smile, you actually release positive endorphins throughout your body. By observing your reflection *and smiling*, you are teaching your mouth what to do, just as God's Word says. And the more you teach it how to respond, the more you will be able to maintain peace in difficult times.

Yield to His Powerful Presence Within You

Let's look once more at our opening Scripture in James. It says:

Even so the tongue is a little member and boasts great things. See how great a forest a little fire kindles!
—James 3:5

The next verse goes on to say that the tongue itself is a fire, a world of iniquity, and one translation says it can turn our whole lives into a blazing flame of destruction and disaster (*see* James 3:6 *TLB*). The tongue is so powerful in the way it can govern your life, but with the help of the Holy Spirit inside you, you can allow it to direct your life according to the Word of God.

Rather than give in to your thoughts or emotions, reflect on how you want your life to turn out. Remember when Jesus was reviled and insulted, He did not respond in the same way. His Word tells us that we are blessed when people speak evil towards us because of His Kingdom, so allow His Spirit to guide you in your response and before you know it, you will be walking in His peace each and every day (*see* Matthew 5:11).

Denise's prayer for you:

Father God, right now we come before You in the name of Jesus, and we thank You for the power of the Holy Spirit on the inside of us. We come in agreement with the fruit of self-control within us and because of that we can exercise power over our tongue. Lord, help us to remember that to maintain peace in these difficult times, it is so important to reflect on our words and choose words of life in every situation. I pray this in the powerful, wonderful name of Jesus. Amen.

STUDY QUESTIONS

Be diligent to present yourself approved to God, a worker
who does not need to be ashamed, rightly dividing the word of truth.
— 2 Timothy 2:15

1. The Bible has much to say about the words we speak. According to Psalm 34:11-13 and First Peter 3:8-12, how are our words connected with the reverential fear of the Lord?

2. What did David ask the Lord to do for him regarding his mouth in Psalm 141:3?

3. What do Proverbs 13:3 and 21:23 say are the benefits of guarding your mouth?

PRACTICAL APPLICATION

But be doers of the word,
and not hearers only, deceiving yourselves.
— James 1:22

1. When it comes to verbally interacting with others, how are you doing? Take a few moments to ask yourself these questions and answer honestly:

    • *Am I quick to listen and slow to speak?*

    • *Am I quick to get angry or do I control my temper?*

    • *Are my words nourishing or poisoning to others and to my own soul?*

    • *What kind of "fruit" am I reaping from the seed of my words?*

    • How do you think the people closest to you would answer these same questions about you?

    • Do you need help in controlling your mouth? God stands ready, willing, and able to transform the way you speak and interact with others. Get quiet in His presence and begin to pray, "Lord, please forgive me for my harsh, hurtful responses and for not controlling my words. Teach me how to be slow to speak, quick to listen, and quick to turn to You for help when I'm confronted with heated, abrasive words. Help me to give a gentle answer in every situation and respond as Jesus would. In His name I pray, amen!"

TOPIC
Maintaining Peace by Controlling Your Mouth AGAIN

SCRIPTURES

1. **Proverbs 18:8,20** — The words of a talebearer are like tasty trifles, and they go down into the inmost body. A man's stomach shall be satisfied from the fruit of his mouth; from the produce of his lips he shall be filled.

2. **Proverbs 16:24** — Pleasant words are like a honeycomb, sweetness to the soul and health to the bones.

3. **Proverbs 21:23** — Whoever guards his mouth and tongue keeps his soul from troubles.

4. **Proverbs 19:13** — A foolish son is the ruin of his father, and the contentions of a wife are a continual dripping.

5. **Philippians 2:14,15** — Do all things without complaining and disputing, that you may become blameless and harmless, children of God without fault in the midst of a crooked and perverse generation, among whom you shine as lights in the world.

SYNOPSIS

In our previous lesson, we talked a great deal about the power of our words and how one of the greatest ways we can maintain peace is by controlling our mouth. What you choose to say can either ignite a fire in a situation or usher in God's peace. The Bible confirms this by saying, "A gentle answer deflects anger, but harsh words make tempers flare" (*see* Proverbs 15:1 *NLT*).

Keeping a guard on one's mouth is an indicator of true maturity. The Bible says, "We all stumble in many ways. Anyone who is never at fault in what they say is perfect, able to keep their whole body in check" (*see* James 3:2 *NIV*). By learning to tame our tongue through the empowerment of the Holy Spirit, we can eliminate many problems and maintain peace even in difficult situations.

The emphasis of this lesson:

God doesn't want us to use our mouths for gossip, complaining, or contentious speech. He wants us to use our words to speak life and health to others and to ourselves. In our previous lesson, we learned that our inward man is either nourished or poisoned by the words we speak. We can avoid a great deal of grief before it starts by guarding what comes out of our mouth.

Gossip Is Evil and Grieves God's Heart

One of the challenges we face when it comes to controlling our mouth is the issue of *gossip*. The Bible has a great deal to say about this subject, especially in the book of Proverbs. One Scripture that mentions this is found in Proverbs 18:8. It says, "The words of a talebearer are like tasty trifles, and they go down into the inmost body." In this verse, the writer classifies gossip as *talebearing*. One definition of a talebearer is *one who maliciously gossips or reveals secrets.*

Do you know someone who is recognized as a gossiper? They reveal things about others that is not their place to share. Even Christians can fall into this trap, sharing intimate, often hurtful or embarrassing details about other individuals, under the guise of a "prayer request." They say, "Oh, so-and-so really needs prayer. I heard that they were doing such-and-such, and it's really a sad situation. We really need to pray for them."

If you have ever found out pieces of information about someone that you would really like to tell others, don't give in to that temptation. For one thing, if that person told you in confidence, you will betray their trust in you. And if the information about someone came second-hand, many times it is not even true or certainly not the full story. It is gossip, and it is a terrible thing to be a part of because it destroys people's lives. In fact, Hebrew scholars tell us that spreading gossip is like killing a person in the following three ways:

1. The person doesn't know what is being said about them.

2. The person can't defend themselves.
3. The person is being cursed repeatedly in the ears of others.

Make no mistake, gossip is evil, and we don't want to have anything to do with it.

What Kind of 'Produce' Is Filling Your Belly?

What many don't realize is that when a person gossips, it affects the gossiper first. Again, it says that the words of a talebearer go down into the inmost body. So, when gossip leaves a person's lips, Scripture says it goes down into their belly or inward man. This understanding is echoed and expanded on in Proverbs 18:20, which says:

A man's stomach shall be satisfied from the fruit of his mouth; from the produce of his lips he shall be filled.

This verse says we are filled with what we are producing from our own lips. That means the gossiper is eating the lying, slanderous words he or she is speaking. Their words are also going down into *their* spirit, their inward man. This sobering truth should make all of us stop and seriously think about what we are saying. The Bible says that the Lord shines His light on a person's spirit and searches all the inner depths of their heart (*see* Proverbs 20:27). Do we really want those types of words coming out of our mouth to go into our spirit?

If we are honest, none of us want words of criticism or faultfinding to be planted in our hearts, so we need to refrain from speaking them. Instead, we should be speaking words of blessing and peace — the same kinds of words we would want others to say about us.

Just because you heard something about someone else doesn't mean you should share it, and again, keep in mind, it may not fully be true. We usually know on the inside when we should refrain from disclosing something about another person — especially if we are walking in relationship with God. If we don't want to eat the words we are about to say, we shouldn't say them. Yet one more reason to exercise the fruit of self-control and be slow to speak.

Kind Words Produce Healthy Bodies

Now that we know a little bit about the effects of slanderous words, let's see what the Word of God says about positive words that produce life. It tells us in Proverbs 16:24, "Pleasant words are like a honeycomb, sweetness to the soul and health to the bones." This is not just a metaphorical statement, because the Bible is absolute truth.

When you speak kind and loving words to and about others, it is like partaking honey, and it brings a delight to your own soul. As a matter of fact, it has so much impact, the Bible says it brings health to the bones. You can have stronger bones just by your own words!

You can promote health in others and in your own body by speaking words of life. Words that are pleasant and uplifting can impart grace and kindness to a person's soul and health to the strongest part of the human body — the bones. You have the power to impart life to others just by the very words you speak to them!

Another Scripture that reveals this truth from a different aspect, is found in Proverbs 21:23. It says, "Whoever guards his mouth and tongue keeps his soul from troubles." *Guarding* the words that are coming out of our mouth is another way we can keep our soul from distress. How many times have we regretted something we said and made a mess of things? Thankfully, if we will guard our words with the help of the Holy Spirit living inside us, we can put a stop to a great deal of grief before it starts.

Contentious Words Are Like a Dripping Faucet

Scripture also provides us insight into words spoken in our closest relationships. The book of Proverbs was mostly written by King Solomon; his great wisdom came from God and he was both a husband and a father. It tells us in Proverbs 19:13, "A foolish son is the ruin of his father, and the contentions of a wife are a continual dripping." Notice the word *contentions* — it means to be *antagonistic, combative, belligerent* and *given to provoking an argument.*

If you are a wife, God is trying to help you see how your words and the attitude in which you speak can affect your husband. If you are contentious — argumentative, difficult, trying to correct him all the time — the Bible says you are like a "continual dripping." Have you ever had a faucet that wouldn't stop dripping? In just a short time, the sound became annoying and you wanted to turn it off. In the same way, if you are contentious with your husband, on the inside he wants to turn *you* off.

The Russian translation of this verse is even more descriptive. Basically, it says that a woman who is contentious is like *running sewage*. Who wants to be around sewage? People build piping systems to capture sewage and transport it far away. No one plans a picnic where there is running sewage. The smell is overwhelmingly offensive, and no one wants to be linked to it in any way.

Just as no one wants to be associated with sewage, no one wants to be associated with or stained by a faultfinding, criticizing, contentious person. If you're letting argumentative and combative words regularly come out of your mouth, it is like you are expelling raw sewage — and your attitude has an aroma that makes people, including your spouse, want to get away from you.

If this seems to describe you, don't feel condemned. Instead, receive these warnings from Scripture as divine instruction on what you need to change in your life. God is not mad at you, He loves you, and He is more than able to help you change the way you speak when you follow the guidelines in His Word (*see* Ephesians 4:29-32, John 14:26).

It is important to note this passage is *not* saying you should never communicate your concerns and feelings to your husband. It is healthy to share your heart respectfully with him. What this verse is identifying as annoying is a regular habit of complaining or faultfinding, and making sure we don't have a hidden motive to manipulate him to see or do things our way.

Thankfully, we have the power of the Holy Spirit inside us to help us revamp our vocabulary. We can begin to pray, "Father God, I yield my whole self to Your Spirit within me which includes my tongue. I want the words of my mouth to be like honey and communicate the fragrance of God instead of the revolting smell of sewage. Help me to do what Your Word says and empower me to think and speak as Jesus would. I ask this in Jesus' name, amen!"

We Are To Do Everything Without Complaining

What else does God say about the words of our mouth? Philippians 2:14 tells us, "Do all things without complaining and disputing." One commentary's definition of the word "complaining" is defined as *murmuring; an expression of dissatisfaction*. It goes on to say complaining is *grumbling* or *muttering in a low voice*; it is a kind of grumbling that promotes ill will instead of harmony and goodwill. Moreover, it's *a questioning, a dispute, a discussion; a skeptical questioning or criticism*. Interestingly, this dissatisfaction begins on the inside long before it finds its way into our words.

Many times, people may not verbalize something out loud but they are having a conversation on the inside. It is an internal voice that repeatedly says, *I don't like this, I don't like that, why are they telling me to do this? Oh, I can't believe they did that and I just cannot stand it any longer!* You can tell something is going on with them through their emotions, their actions, and sometimes their words. Complaining is like having an upset stomach that remains in turmoil, producing a continual discontent. It is this kind of attitude that the Word of God warns us not to practice because He has called us to peace.

When the apostle Paul wrote this command under the inspiration of the Holy Spirit he was incarcerated in one of the worst prisons ever. While he had every reason to murmur and complain because of the horrible conditions he was in, he didn't. Instead, he chose to have an attitude of gratitude and keep a godly perspective on the inside of him. While most people would have used their mouth to complain about the circumstances, Paul guarded his mouth and penned the powerful book of Philippians that included the exhortation to rejoice always (*see* Philippians 4:4).

When We Control Our Mouths, We Shine Brightly in This Dark World

Complaining is not beneficial for any person to practice, but there is also a reward for avoiding it, and it is found in the very next verse. As we just read in Philippians 2:14, the apostle Paul charged us to do all things without complaining and disputing. Verse 15 continues on to say:

> **That you may become blameless and harmless, children of God without fault in the midst of a crooked and perverse generation, among whom you shine as lights in the world.**
> **— Philippians 2:15**

When we choose *not* to complain, and instead maintain our peace, God says we are blameless and harmless, without fault in the midst of a crooked and perverse generation. We become shining stars to the world around us that light the way to God's Kingdom.

What a great testimony for someone to consider you blameless or harmless! It will cause people to be drawn towards you, because they will not be concerned you will say something that will belittle or condemn them. This verse says that you will be a shining example of what it means to be a child of God, when you do things without complaining or arguing.

The fact is there are countless things going on in our culture right now for which we could complain and be upset about. Friend, in this day and hour, your witness is needed! There are people all around you who are incredibly troubled and looking for answers — answers you have in Jesus. We do not want our own mouth to make us appear harmful so that people won't receive from us. If you're frustrated and dissatisfied, spend time in the Word and in prayer and renew your mind to what it says (*see* Romans 12:2). Ask the Holy Spirit to help you put an end to complaining and murmuring and give you specific answers for those who are in desperate need.

If you are feeling convicted of some of these things, please keep in mind there is no condemnation for those who are in Christ Jesus (*see* Romans 8:1). Even the apostle Paul wrote in Philippians chapter 3, that he was still pressing forward — he had not reached the goal of living a perfect Christian life, but he chose to forget his past mistakes and press on to advance the Kingdom of God. Only Jesus is perfect, but that is why He sent the Holy Spirit to be our Helper in every area of our lives. If we will reach out to Him, He will help us change our words and govern our lives in a way that promotes peace within ourselves but also to those around us.

Denise's prayer for you:

Father, I thank You for my friends that are reading this. Right now, I proclaim Your Word that says there is no condemnation in Christ Jesus and no one is being condemned by the truths I am sharing from the Word of God. You are simply giving us instruction and we are declaring right now that we will listen to the Holy Spirit on the inside of us.

We will receive Your answer for conflict and turmoil. When we are tempted to gossip or complain, we will look for the right words on the inside from the Holy Spirit who is our Helper, the Spirit of Truth. We thank You for the right things to say to a troubled world so we can shine like stars, and maintain peace in difficult times. We love You and thank You so much for Your Word. In Jesus' name. Amen.

STUDY QUESTIONS

**Be diligent to present yourself approved to God, a worker
who does not need to be ashamed, rightly dividing the word of truth.
— 2 Timothy 2:15**

1. The Bible says in Proverbs 16:24, "Pleasant words are like a honeycomb, sweetness to the soul and health to the bones." How does this help you better understand Psalm 119:103 and Jeremiah 15:16? Have you ever looked at Scripture in this way? (Also consider 1 Peter 2:2, Job 23:12, and Deuteronomy 8:3.)

2. The Holy Spirit gives us some powerful instruction about our words. Take some time to carefully read what he wrote in the following verses, and in your own words, describe what they are speaking to your own heart.
   - Ephesians 4:25,29-32
   - Colossians 4:5,6
   - Titus 3:1,2

PRACTICAL APPLICATION

**But be doers of the word,
and not hearers only, deceiving yourselves.
— James 1:22**

1. Can you recall a situation in which you were acting ungodly, and someone treated you just like Jesus — speaking kind and pleasant words in response that you didn't deserve? How did their words affect you? And how did those words affect your perception of that person?

2. Have you ever been the one to speak kind and loving words to someone who didn't deserve it? What kind of an impact did your words have? How did the experience impact you?

3. Are you guilty of using your mouth to gossip, be contentious, or complain? God does not condemn you, He just wants you to come to Him and surrender yourself in prayer. Humble your heart before the Lord and say, "Lord, I know my attitude is wrong and my mouth has

voiced much negativity. Please forgive me for _____ and wash me clean with the blood of Jesus (*see* 1 John 1:7,9). Holy Spirit, remind me of the truths I have learned and help me walk in them. I want to be blameless and harmless, a shining example of what it means to be a child of God to the darkness around me. In Jesus' name. Amen!"

TOPIC

Maintaining Peace by Remembering What God Has Already Done for You

SCRIPTURES

1. **Acts 7:59,60** — …He was calling on God and saying, "Lord Jesus, receive my spirit." Then he knelt down and cried out with a loud voice, "Lord, do not charge them with this sin." And when he had said this, he fell asleep.

2. **Luke 23:34** — Then Jesus said, "Father, forgive them, for they do not know what they do." And they divided His garments and cast lots.

3. **John 16:13** — However, when He, the Spirit of truth, has come, He will guide you into all truth; for He will not speak on His own authority, but whatever He hears He will speak; and He will tell you things to come.

4. **Psalm 139:13** — For You formed my inward parts; You covered me in my mother's womb.

5. **James 5:16** — Confess your trespasses to one another, and pray for one another, that you may be healed. The effective, fervent prayer of a righteous man avails much.

6. **James 1:2** — My brethren, count it all joy when you fall into various trials.

7. **Matthew 11:28-30** — Come to Me, all you who labor and are heavy laden, and I will give you rest. Take My yoke upon you and learn from Me, for I am gentle and lowly in heart, and you will find rest for your souls. For My yoke is easy and My burden is light.

8. **Matthew 6:34** — Therefore do not worry about tomorrow, for tomorrow will worry about its own things. Sufficient for the day is its own trouble.

9. **Psalm 103:1-3** — Bless the Lord, O my soul; and all that is within me, bless His holy name! Bless the Lord, O my soul, and forget not all His benefits: Who forgives all your iniquities, Who heals all your diseases.

SYNOPSIS

Peace is priceless. We can have material possessions, plenty of money, a wonderful job, and great friends, but without peace, it's really challenging to enjoy anything. That's why the Bible tells us to "…Search for peace (harmony; undisturbedness from fears, agitating passions, and moral conflicts) and seek it eagerly. [Do not merely desire peaceful relations with God, with your fellowmen, and with yourself, but pursue, go after them!]" (*see* 1 Peter 3:11 *AMPC*).

So far, we have explored many things that we can do to maintain peace in difficult times. All of them involve digging into God's Word, staying humbly connected in fellowship with Him, and surrendering ourselves and our circumstances to the abiding presence and power of the Holy Spirit within us. In this final lesson, we will review what we've learned and discover the importance of remembering what God has already done for us.

The emphasis of this lesson:

Remembering how God helped you in the past strengthens you to trust Him to help you in the present and the future. Whatever you're facing right now, you can maintain peace knowing that He will come through for you again.

14 THINGS TO HELP YOU MAINTAIN PEACE IN DIFFICULT TIMES

1) The Power of Forgiveness

The Word of God clearly shows us how the power of forgiveness can affect our lives and the lives of those around us. Many times, when we are having difficulty with others, what they did to us becomes so magnified in our eyes that we can't see our own fault in the situation. Hurt by their mistreatment, we begin to hold onto their offense and the hurt we've experienced, which often produces negative side effects. That is exactly what happened to Denise many years ago. Here's what she shared:

> Many years ago, I became offended, and I didn't quite know how to handle it. As I was seeking the Lord, I began to have symptoms in my body. My hands and feet were painfully cold all the time, and I was also having panic attacks. Even worse, great fear was gripping my heart and my mind, so much that I would go to bed and wake up with it. It felt like there was a vice on my mind. Day after day, I tried to find an answer for why I was in so much pain, not realizing it was due to the unforgiveness in my heart.
>
> *If this person would just change*, I thought, *Everything would be okay*. So, I just kept seeking the Lord and seeking the Lord, but nothing changed. Then I came to a place where I was so desperate for an answer from God, I remember grabbing hold of the sink one night, and I said, 'God, I don't know what's going on in my life. The pain and panic I'm dealing with is so terrible. You know my struggle, Lord, and I'm not letting go of You until this is resolved.'
>
> About 2 weeks later, I was in a service, and a prophet spoke over me. Although he knew nothing about me or what I was dealing with, he looked at me and said, 'You are a very sensitive person, and you have broken places in your heart. But in 24 hours, you're going to wake up in a different world.'
>
> Sure enough, within 24 hours, I was able to see that my problem was not the other person — it was me. I was responsible for my own heart and needed to forgive them and surrender the situation into God's hands. So that is what I did.
>
> I went to sleep, and in the middle of the night, God reached His invisible hand inside me and took away all the horrible bitterness, resentment, and unforgiveness. He cut all the tentacles that went down into my soul that were causing me panic and fear. The next morning when I woke up, it was as if I was in a different world, just like the prophet had said. My hands and feet were completely healed, and most importantly my mind was completely peaceful.

Friend, if we want to maintain peace in difficult times, we must recognize offense and unforgiveness that is trying to lodge in our heart and make the choice to forgive. A perfect example of choosing to forgive others is found in the life of one of the early disciples. Stephen was powerfully testifying that Jesus is the Messiah, and as the Jewish leaders were stoning him because of it, Acts 7:59 and 60 says:

> …He was calling on God and saying, "Lord Jesus, receive my spirit." Then he knelt down and cried out with a loud voice, "Lord, do not charge them with this sin." And when he had said this, he fell asleep.

Through his words in that moment, Stephen released any offense he may have had towards the people from what they did to him. What's interesting is in that crowd of religious leaders was a man named Saul, who later became the apostle Paul. What would have happened had Stephen not released forgiveness over them? Would we have an apostle Paul? Would we have two-thirds of the New Testament that he wrote?

In John 20:23, Jesus said, "If you forgive the sins of any, they are forgiven them; if you retain the sins of any, they are retained." Stephen forgave the sins of the religious leaders, asking God not to hold their offensive actions against them. It is the same thing Jesus prayed for everyone who participated in His crucifixion. While He was hanging on the Cross, He prayed:

> …Father, forgive them, for they do not know what they do….
> — Luke 23:34

Forgiveness is the attitude of Heaven toward all offenders. By God's grace, we can say, "Lord, please don't hold this against them. Forgive them because they don't know what they're doing." As we choose to forgive our offenders, God will continue to extend His forgiveness to us, enabling us to maintain peace in the middle of difficult situations.

2) Controlling Your Emotions

God has given us the power, through His Spirit within us, to handle our emotions in a stable and godly way. In Psalm 139:13, David wrote about God's involvement in our creation, saying, "For You formed my inward parts; You covered me in my mother's womb." God designed and created every part of us, including our emotions, so there is nothing wrong with having them. Where we get into trouble is when we allow them to control us. By God's grace, we can learn to run to Him when we're feeling over-whelmed and receive His strength to manage our emotions through the power of the Holy Spirit.

3) Choosing To Be Thankful

One of the best things we can do when disappointments and difficulties set in is to purposely begin thanking God for the many good things He has done in our life. Psalm 100:4 (*AMPC*) instructs us, "Enter into His gates with thanksgiving and a thank offering and into His courts with praise! Be thankful and say so to Him, bless and affectionately praise His name!"

On the program, Denise shared how many years ago, she and her husband Rick, started a church in the United States but they were out of the will of God. Consequently, they became very poor and at one point, they were so broke that there was no food in their refrigerator for them and their first son, Paul, who was just about two years old.

At the time, Denise was reading a book titled "You Get What You Say," and there was an example in it of a man who had the same problem — an empty refrigerator. The book stated how this man began passing his refrigerator every day, praising God for his fridge being filled with food.

Denise thought about it and decided to do the same thing. So, each time she walked by their empty refrigerator, instead of focusing on what she saw and getting depressed, she would say, "I praise You, Lord, I praise You!," thanking Him for food. Sure enough, after several days, someone came and filled their refrigerator with food!

It's easy to recognize the bad going on around us; anyone can do that. It takes the wisdom of God and a commitment to maintain peace in difficult times to recognize the good. When troubles come, pray and ask God for His grace to choose to be thankful and remember all of the good He has done.

4) Seeing Your Problem As Smaller Than God

It is important to always keep our focus on *how great our God is*, rather than what we see in front of us. Whatever has our attention and what we keep talking about, or *magnify*, tends to grow bigger and bigger in our eyes. When David confronted Goliath, that is what he focused on, *the greatness of God*, not the size of the giant. As a result, he ran toward Goliath unintimidated, with confidence in the power of the Lord. He knew the importance of seeing his problem as smaller than God. It's likely why he wrote in Psalm 34:3, "Oh, magnify the Lord with me, and let us exalt His name together." One way we can hold on to peace is by learning to see God as bigger than our problem and our problem as smaller than God.

5) Knowing the Lover on the Inside

Knowing the love that God has just for *you*, and that He lives in you, is a key part in strengthening and empowering you to rest in His protection, remain calm, and take authority over the enemy's attacks. The Bible tells us again and again that you are the temple of the Holy Spirit. Your body is His house (*see* John 14:16,17; 1 Corinthians 6:19). The moment you received Jesus as your Lord and Savior, the Holy Spirit came to take up permanent residence in your heart. He is the powerful third person of the Godhead, and the character and nature of who He is exists inside you in seed form (*see* Galatians 5:22,23). If you will listen and pay attention to Him, He will bring that calm to the middle of life's storms and help you maintain peace in difficult times.

6) Knowing the Comforter

In John 14:16 (*KJV*), Jesus said, "And I will pray the Father, and he shall give you another Comforter, that he may abide with you for ever." As your Comforter, the Holy Spirit was sent to you to walk alongside you, giving you the counsel, encouragement, and direction you need in every situation you face.

Jesus also said in John 16:13, "…When He, the Spirit of truth, has come, He will guide you into all truth; for He will not speak on His own authority, but whatever He hears He will speak; and He will tell you things to come." Whenever we are challenged and don't know what to do, rather than get upset and lose our peace, we can ask the Holy Spirit, and He will teach us what to do (*see* 1 John 2:27). He lives inside us and stands ready, willing, and able at all times to help with anything we are facing.

7) Refusing the Trap of Isolation

The Bible says that our enemy, the devil, looks around for someone to devour (*see* 1 Peter 5:8). When we are struggling with things like persistent fear, recurring sin, or a prolonged state of sadness, we are often tempted to separate ourselves by disconnecting from others — either partially or completely. The devil wants to trap us and keep us isolated by telling us that what we are dealing with is unique to us, and no one will understand what we are going through.

It turns out that the very opposite is true. James 5:16 says:

> **Confess your trespasses to one another, and pray for one another, that you may be healed….**

When you humble yourself and share with a trusted friend what you have been walking through, you bring the problem out of darkness and into the light of truth. No problem or hurt is too hopeless for Jesus to handle! Even if you feel you are at your lowest point and have hit "rock bottom," there is still hope. Open your heart to the Lord and find a trustworthy, godly friend you can confide in. Healing will begin to flood your mind and heart.

8) Making a Habit of Rejoicing

One of the most powerful things we can do in times of difficulty is to choose the joy that is already residing within us by the power of the Holy Spirit. Even when you don't *feel* happy or joyful, there is still joy in your heart because it is a fruit of the Spirit, and He is in you.

Through James, the half-brother of Jesus, the Lord tells us to "…count it all joy when you fall into various trials" (*see* James 1:2). When we choose to rejoice in spite of a test or trial, we are opening the door to God's power. Choosing joy generates a type of power that helps you hold on and hang in there regardless of what is happening around you.

9) Giving Your Worries to God

Another important part of maintaining peace is choosing to cast our cares on the Lord. Because He loves us and promised to take care of us, we can trust Him to watch over us. Jesus said in Matthew 11:28-30:

> **Come to Me, all you who labor and are heavy laden, and I will give you rest. Take My yoke upon you and learn from Me, for I am gentle and lowly in heart, and you will find rest for your souls. For My yoke is easy and My burden is light.**

Jesus doesn't want us carrying a heavy load that keeps us overwhelmed with hardship and exhaustion. He wants us to come and give that to Him so He can take care of us. We need to remember that we are not the one with the answer but *He is*, and we must realize that *before* we can cast our care. He is the One who sent the Holy Spirit. He is the One who lives on the inside of us and who is our Helper. We may have many questions, but He always has the exact answer we need.

If we feel weary and heavy laden with worry and responsibility, we need to come to Jesus — recognizing that He alone is our answer — cast our care upon Him, and we will find rest in His loving presence.

10) Recognizing the Real Enemy

Because we deal with people on a regular basis, there are often conflicts and misunderstandings that arise. It can be easy to look at the person in front of us and lose our peace, thinking that they are the ones we are fighting with when in reality, our enemy is much more sinister and much less visible than we realize. Our fight is not with the people around us. Our fight is with our enemy, Satan, and the spirits of darkness we don't see.

The apostle Paul elaborates on this truth in Ephesians 6:12, where he wrote:

> **For we do not wrestle against flesh and blood, but against principalities, against powers, against the rulers of the darkness of this age, against spiritual hosts of wickedness in the heavenly places.**

Don't waste your time and energy fighting against someone who is not your enemy — you won't win. Your fight is a spiritual one and there is no reason for you to be intimidated. The Bible says you are seated in Heavenly places with Christ *far above* your enemies. You have the Greater One on the inside of you and the authority to come against anything that's coming against you in the name of Jesus!

11) Living One Day at a Time

God's supernatural power is available to you to do anything He has called you to do — but the amount we need is only given one day at a time. Jesus said it this way:

Therefore do not worry about tomorrow, for tomorrow will worry about its own things. Sufficient for the day is its own trouble.

— Matthew 6:34

If anyone could have worried about tomorrow, it would have been Jesus, and He is our example. He faced many difficult challenges throughout His life, but He lived in the grace and power He was given, one day at a time.

Friend, there is great courage and strength in waking up every morning and giving your entire attention to what is before you just in that day. He promises to give you the grace — His supernatural power — to live one day at a time, and it is this mindset that enables you to maintain peace, even in difficult times.

12) Guarding Your Thoughts

Romans 12:2 tells us that we should renew our minds according to the Word of God, and wrong thinking is one of the main reasons for a lack of peace. The enemy seeks to build strongholds of ungodly thoughts in our mind, but we can destroy those strongholds by using the powerful spiritual weapons God has given us.

Second Corinthians 10:4 says, "For the weapons of our warfare are not carnal but mighty in God for pulling down strongholds." We were just reminded that our fight is not with what we see in this natural realm, but with evil spirits we don't see. The weapons we have been given to fight all of our battles, including the ones in our mind, are spiritual ones, and mighty for fighting in that realm.

Instead of passively receiving every thought that comes into your mind, recognize and reject wrong thoughts that don't belong. This is done by resisting those thoughts and throwing them away before the seed of it can take root in your soul (*see* 2 Corinthians 10:5).

In addition to taking a defensive stand against ungodly thoughts, we are also to take an *offensive* approach. This is revealed in Philippians 4:8, where the apostle Paul said:

Finally, brethren, whatever things are true, whatever things are noble, whatever things are just, whatever things are pure, whatever things are lovely, whatever things are of good report,

if there is any virtue and if there is anything praiseworthy — meditate on these things.

No matter where you are in your walk with God, you can probably find at least one thing to think about in each of these eight categories. By choosing to think on these kinds of things rather than wrong thoughts, your mind and heart will stay peaceful, even in difficult times.

13) Controlling Your Mouth

The mouth is a small part of the body but despite its size, it packs great power. The Bible says in Proverbs 18:21 that death and life are in the power of the tongue. In other words, the words we speak are either going to bring blessing or destruction upon our lives and the lives of others.

Friend, God doesn't want us to use our mouth for gossip, complaining, or contentious speech. He wants us to use our words to speak life and health to others and to ourselves. Remember, the words we speak about others will fill us also (*see* Proverbs 18:8,20). We can avoid a great deal of grief before it starts by guarding what comes out of our mouth.

With the help of the Holy Spirit, we can control our mouth by studying and reflecting on what to say before we say it, being quick to hear, slow to speak and slow to become angry. We can speak words that are pleasant to the hearer, spreading the fragrance of God through those words, so that we shine like stars in this dark world that is looking for answers (*see* 2 Corinthians 2:14-17, Philippians 2:14-15). When you allow the Holy Spirit to guide you and use your words to impart life and health to others, it will be easier to walk in His peace each and every day.

14) Remembering What God Has Already Done for You

Let's look at one more way to maintain peace in difficult times, and that is purposefully remembering what God has already done for us. In Scripture, someone who modeled this practice very well was David, and he writes about it in Psalm 103. He begins his song with these words:

Bless the Lord, O my soul; and all that is within me, bless His holy name!

Bless the Lord, O my soul, and forget not all His benefits:

Who forgives all your iniquities, Who heals all your diseases,

Who redeems your life from destruction, Who crowns you with lovingkindness and tender mercies,

Who satisfies your mouth with good things, so that your youth is renewed like the eagle's.

— Psalm 103:1-5

Notice that the words of this song he had written spoke directly to his own soul — his mind, will, and emotions — and they reminded him to bless the Lord with everything he had inside him. David also told his soul *not to forget all of God's benefits* (v. 2). There is power in remembering all the things God has done in your life! This was not a new concept for David — this was something he already practiced. Before he went out to face the giant Goliath, he recounted to King Saul the fact that God had given him the ability to kill both a lion and a bear that were trying to devour his sheep (*see* 1 Samuel 17:34-37). And because God had already proven Himself faithful, David knew that God would be faithful again.

Hebrews 13:8 says that Jesus is the same yesterday, today, and forever, so He is not going to change. If you are facing another problem right now, be at peace and remain calm. He has directed your steps and delivered you before, and He will be faithful to do it again. He is Almighty God, and His power has not diminished one bit!

Take time regularly to remember what God did for you in the past. And say to whatever it is you are facing, "God delivered me before, and He will certainly do it again!"

Denise's prayer for you:

> Father, You know what is going on inside every person. You know whatever struggle that person might be dealing with, whatever pressure the enemy is applying, trying to steal their peace. And Father, I thank You that Greater is the One that is on the inside of them than the one that is in this world trying to bring them down. Help them to remember Your goodness and faithfulness in their lives. I thank You for Your power that is fully present to encourage and strengthen them at this time. I pray this in the mighty, wonderful name of Jesus, amen.

Friend, don't you just love the Word of God; it is so powerful and packed with instruction and encouragement. The Holy Spirit is right there with you; whatever it is that you are facing just receive His touch right now, because His presence is hovering over you to impart that peace and strength to you.

Anytime you are facing challenges in life, remind yourself of the truths you have learned in these lessons, because each one will help you walk in victory and continue to maintain peace in difficult times.

STUDY QUESTIONS

**Be diligent to present yourself approved to God, a worker
who does not need to be ashamed, rightly dividing the word of truth.
— 2 Timothy 2:15**

1. When God sent His angels to announce the birth of Jesus, what were they declaring as they were praising God (*see* Luke 2:14)? And what was the first thing Jesus told His disciples when He appeared to them after His resurrection (*see* John 20:19)? What does that tell you about how the presence of Jesus influences our ability to maintain peace in difficult times?

2. When we operate in the wisdom found in God's Word, Scripture says it will add peace to our lives (*see* Proverbs 3:1,2; Psalm 119:165). Also considering James 3:17 and 18, what else stands out to you about the connection between *peace* and *wisdom*? According to Psalm 34:11-14 and First Peter 3:10 and 11, what is the reward of continuing to pursue peace?

3. Read the following passages in different Bible versions — Numbers 6:24-26, Psalm 4:8 and 29:11, Isaiah 26:3, Romans 8:6, Ephesians 2:14, and Second Thessalonians 3:16. Which ones about peace really resonate with your heart? Invest some time and write them out on a sheet of paper, displaying it where you will see and read it regularly. There's so much power in reminding ourselves of God's Word!

PRACTICAL APPLICATION

**But be doers of the word,
and not hearers only, deceiving yourselves.**
—James 1:22

1. As you review and reflect on this series, which biblical story, scripture, or personal story from Denise impacted you the most? What made it significant for you? Which challenges that were described sound most like the season of life you are experiencing at the moment?

2. Of all the truths explored in these lessons, which one has stayed with you the most? Which one have you started to put into practice and which one could you use some help with?

3. Take some time to think about what it would be like to maintain peace while being under pressure. How do you want your heart, your spirit, to handle situations you may be facing? Invite the Holy Spirit to strengthen your inward man as you begin to take the steps we've learned about. Remember that God is able to do exceedingly abundantly above all that we ask or think, according to the power that works in us (*see* Ephesians 3:20).

A Prayer To Receive Salvation

If you've never received Jesus as your Savior and Lord, now is the time for you to experience the new life Jesus wants to give you! To receive God's gift of salvation that can be obtained through Jesus alone, pray this prayer from your heart:

Jesus, I repent of my sin and receive You as my Savior and Lord. Wash away my sin with Your precious blood and make me completely new. I thank You that my sin is removed, and Satan no longer has any right to lay claim on me. Through Your empowering grace, I faithfully promise that I will serve You as my Lord for the rest of my life.

If you just prayed this prayer of salvation, you are born again! You are a brand-new creation in Christ! Would you please let us know of your decision by going to **renner.org/salvation**? We would love to connect with you and pray for you as you begin your new life in Christ.

Scriptures for further study: John 3:16; John 14:6; Acts 4:12; Ephesians 1:7; Hebrews 10:19,20; 1 Peter 1:18,19; Romans 10:9,10; Colossians 1:13; 2 Corinthians 5:17; Romans 6:4; 1 Peter 1:3

Notes

CLAIM YOUR FREE RESOURCE!

As a way of introducing you further to the teaching ministry of Rick Renner, we would like to send you FREE of charge his teaching, "How To Receive a Miraculous Touch From God" on CD or as an MP3 download.

In His earthly ministry, Jesus commonly healed *all* who were sick of *all* their diseases. In this profound message, learn about the manifold dimensions of Christ's wisdom, goodness, power, and love toward all humanity who came to Him in faith with their needs.

☑ **YES, I want to receive Rick Renner's monthly teaching letter!**

Simply scan the QR code to claim this resource or go to: **renner.org/claim-your-free-offer**

Connect WITH US!

www.ingramcontent.com/pod-product-compliance
Lightning Source LLC
LaVergne TN
LVHW021358080426
835508LV00020B/2338